TRIBAL
CHURCH

STEVE STROOPE

with Kurt Bruner

B&H
PUBLISHING GROUP
Nashville, Tennessee

ISBN: 978-1-4336-7344-3

Published by B&H Publishing Group
Nashville, Tennessee

Dewey Decimal Classification: 254
Subject Heading: LEADERSHIP \ CHURCH \
SMALL GROUPS

3 4 5 6 7 8 9 10 • 17 16 15 14 13

TRIBAL CHURCH

Dedication

To each individual who has faithfully served as a member of the tribe of elders at Lake Pointe over the past two decades. Their wisdom and discernment have made Lake Pointe a more effective church in fulfilling its purpose. Their friendship and encouragement have made it a real joy to serve.

And to my first tribe including my best friend and wife, Marsha; to my two wonderful girls, Rachael and Lydia; to their husbands, Scott and Mason, who were an answer to many years of prayer; and to my grandchildren, Jax, Maleah, Austen, and Boone, who have been four of God's most delightful gifts.

Acknowledgment

Special thanks to Sandra Stanley and Eva Gour, who did the hard work of making my thoughts legible, and to my mentors through the years, whose fingerprints you will find throughout this book: Dr. James Flamming, Bob Shank, Bill Hybels, Rick Warren, and the hundreds of authors who have influenced me through their writings.

Contents

Foreword by Rick Warren

One of the most common mistakes church leaders make is to assume that everyone in a congregation is alike . . . that they all join for the same reason, have identical needs and interests, and have reached the same level of spiritual maturity. This leads to another faulty assumption that "one-size-fits-all" programs and events are all we need to grow. Of course both of these assumptions are nonsense. God has created every person, every family, and every church unique. That's why we can learn something from every model.

Every congregation is a fellowship of fellowships, a communion of communities, a combination of associations, interest groups, and constituencies. Steve Stroope calls them "tribes." Wise leaders learn the identities, interests, and influences of each of these unique tribes. *But how do you do that?* Fortunately, you are holding the answer in your hand right now! Steve Stroope, my life-long friend and partner in ministry, has written THE book on this topic.

I often tell church planters and young pastors, "You don't have enough time to learn everything by personal experience. You must learn from the experiences of others! It's not only wiser and faster, it's a whole lot less painful!" The truth is that we all learn best from *models*, and this book describes a wonderful model that all of us need to learn from.

I guarantee that what you are about to learn is no mere theory. Steve and I have been close friends since serving together as teenagers on youth evangelism teams. Later our two churches began within a year of each other and our ministries have been intertwined ever since. Just months before 9/11 happened, Lake Pointe Church financially sponsored Saddleback's evangelism pastor in a new church plant in Manhattan.

For more than thirty years, I've watched this "Tribal Church" strategy develop in the real life laboratory of Lake Pointe Church. It began in 1979 with just a handful of people, and now this purpose-driven church is one of the largest and most exciting churches in America, attracting more than ten thousand in attendance at its sixteen weekend services. But more to you is this fact: Lake Pointe is a leadership factory, and Steve Stroope can teach you how to raise up leaders too. One of Saddleback's finest staff members, our associate children's minister, was trained by Steve at Lake Pointe Church.

One of the things I love about this book is that it pays attention to details that others often overlook. In today's *more-is-better* mentality, people often miss the importance of small things—in our personal lives, in our families, and in our churches. It seems that everyone wants to serve God in BIG ways, while God is looking for leaders who bring big integrity to the small responsibilities that often go unnoticed.

Others may miss the small things, *but God doesn't!* He is testing your integrity, your obedience, your faith, and your faithfulness. Anytime you see God's public anointing on a "Big L" leader like Steve Stroope, you can always trace it back to integrity in private matters. Godly leaders treat every task as important, every tribe as significant, and every individual as a vital contributor to the family of God.

Listen and learn from the wisdom of this veteran pastor!

Dr. Rick Warren
Saddleback Church
author of *The Purpose Driven Life*

tribe

Noun

a social division in a traditional society consisting of families or communities linked by social, economic, religious, or blood ties, with a common culture and dialect, typically having a recognized leader. —*OXFORD DICTIONARY ONLINE*

"A tribe is a group of people connected to one another, connected to a leader, and connected to an idea."[1]
—SETH GODIN, *TRIBES*

Introduction

On Father's Day in 1979, seven families gathered just out-side of Dallas on the western shore of Lake Ray Hubbard. Although this small fellowship began meeting in a former bait house, they believed God would do mighty things in and through their ministry, which would come to be known as Lake Pointe Church.

Six months later, when I came as their first pastor, they had grown to an average weekly attendance of almost sixty people, if you counted children in the nursery and a small mouse that lived in the upright piano. Thankfully the mouse only made one appearance, scampering across the keys dur-ing the playing of a worship song. To her credit, Joy Brown, our reluctant pianist, never missed a note of the hymn. She had practiced all week long and was not about to let the unin-vited co-accompanist deter her from her task.

By God's grace, Lake Pointe Church has experienced sig-nificant growth since those early days. Today, on an average weekend, four worship bands, one small orchestra, and three lone pianists, accompany close to ten thousand people, wor-shipping in sixteen services in two languages on six different campuses. In addition, over the last ten years Lake Pointe has played a key role in starting a significant church in Las Vegas, Portland, Tampa, Boca Raton, Boston, Fort Smith, Fort Worth, two churches in New York City, and three churches in San Francisco. Last year the people of Lake Pointe gave close to $3.2 million to mission causes all around the world.

The point is not to aspire to be a large church in order to have a big impact. It is rather about being faithful to occupy your present opportunity. It is about yielding your current loaves and fish to His plan. It might be hard to believe, but Lake Pointe did not become what some consider a large church with a worldwide impact by striving to grow big. I believe it is rather ironic that at no time in our thirty-one-year history has Lake Pointe ever set a numerical goal for attendance. Lake Pointe's health and growth, to a large extent, is a result of passionately attending to what some would consider the little details and to the smaller "tribes" that make up our church. In short, Lake Pointe is a tribal church that focuses on leading small to have a big impact for His kingdom. The truth is that we have never considered ourselves to be a large church but rather a beautiful mosaic or collection of small tribes.

Tribal Church: Lead Small, Impact Big

Jesus tells the story of a man who went on a journey and left to three servants three different amounts of resources (Matt. 25:14–30). He entrusted five measures of resources to one servant, he gave two measures to another, and to a final servant he left one measure. They were given time and an opportunity to invest and multiply those resources on behalf of their master. The one with five and the one with two measures both doubled what they had been given. The one with only one measure—by his own admission—squandered the opportunity because of fear. While the fearful servant had his allotment taken away, the master allowed the first two servants to keep their original allotments plus what they had gained. The master celebrated their entrepreneurial efforts and encouraged them to continue their faithful work, saying, "Well done, my good and faithful servant. You have been faithful in handling this small amount, so now I will give you many more responsibilities. Let's celebrate together!" (Matt. 25:23 NLT).

God has entrusted every Christian leader with a measure of resources. Some have been given a stewardship that includes thousands of people and millions of dollars, while others' opportunities are measured by the hundreds of people and thousands of dollars. In God's economy a church's success is not measured by size but rather by their faithfulness. This is the very principle upon which *Tribal Church* is based. In other words, if we ever hope to impact big, we must first learn to occupy the present opportunity God has given, whether large or small.

Whether our membership was in the hundreds or the thousands, we have always seen ourselves as a collection of small tribes seeking to make a big impact on the communities in which we gather. That's why this book is for leaders of small churches, mid-size churches, and massive churches, because every church is made up of tribes. Every church is a tribal church. The question is whether the leaders of the church know they lead a church of tribes and whether they are effectively leading these tribes.

Outline of Book

Since every church, regardless of size, is a tribal church, church leaders must know whom those tribes are and how to relate to them. The book begins by focusing on the foundation of tribal leadership: the leader and his or her family. Next, we look at the key tribes that make up the church: family tribes, small group tribes, leadership tribes, generation tribes, elder tribes, and the tribe that consists of new members. After this, we offer one model for starting new tribes, like new campuses and new church plants. Finally, we conclude with a discussion on effectively reaching out to those who have not yet joined one of your church's tribes.

Leading Small Action Plans

The tribal dynamics at play in every church are often subtle, but they are not insignificant. Understanding and responding to this dynamic continues to transform Lake Pointe Church, and I pray it will enrich your church as well. I am a firm believer that the best way to go big is to start small. That's what tribal church is all about. You have taken an important step by picking up and reading this book. But I encourage you to go a step further by inviting your leadership tribe to work through a process that is designed to help you shrink the enormous task of leading a growing church into bite-sized, manageable steps.

This "rapid innovation" process has been used by my coauthor, Kurt Bruner, to help teams in a variety of contexts—including local church leadership. It includes five steps . . .

Step One: AS IS: Effective strategies begin by clearly defining the current reality. Remember, facts are our friends—even when they make us uncomfortable. We cannot move toward a future goal until we have honestly identified the present situation.

Step Two: COULD BE: Highly creative and innovative teams come up with a hundred decent ideas in order to discover a truly great idea. That is why it is important to block time for the team to do some free-form brainstorming, asking "If money was no obstacle and there were no limitations, what might we do?" Capture every idea, hopefully including some wild and crazy concepts, to fuel and inform the next step.

Step Three: MIGHT BE: Since budget WILL be an obstacle and there are real limitations, the person or team responsible for leading a specific ministry area should craft a "conceptual prototype" that helps clarify what the ideal solution or program might look like. The prototype draws from the best "Could Be" ideas as seen through the lenses of the area leader and summarizes goals and key strategies in a "stick figure" version of the plan. The purpose is to move quickly from blue-sky dreams to a more concrete "What if it looked like this?" model. The leader then invites additional input and fine-tuning from the larger team or supervisor before moving to Step Four.

Step Four: SHOULD BE: During a team session, the assigned leader seeks input and reactions to his prototype.

Unlike the "MIGHT BE" session open to every possibility, the purpose of this session is to honestly assess what is feasible given limited resources, time, and tribe realities. It should also be used to brainstorm potential solutions to any obstacles raised and/or changes that would hit the same goal in a slightly different way. The leader should incorporate ideas from this session before proceeding to Step Five.

Step Five: WILL BE: Finally, the senior leader must approve the resources necessary and assign specific steps to a clear owner who will move the plan forward in the next twelve months. In order to reinforce "leading small," it is wise to call the strategy "Phase One," communicating the expectation the vision will grow and process improve "little by little."

Read each of the chapters in this book with these five steps in mind. To help in that process, we have added questions to the end of each chapter that your team may find helpful as you turn tribal concepts into practical steps for leading small action plans. We have also provided short video segments summarizing the big ideas of each chapter to those who have purchased a book at TribalChurchBook.com.

Chapter One

Self-Leadership

Throughout the Bible we find a pattern where God impacts a key leader before He uses that leader to accomplish greater things with the group he leads. When that one leader becomes aligned with God's vision for His people and confronts those issues that are constraining his leadership potential, positive changes begin to materialize for his tribes.

Before Moses was able to lead a nation of three million made up of the twelve tribes of Israel, he had to have a powerful encounter with the living God. The burning bush had to come before the exodus. Thus, the first step of Israel's forty-year journey from slavery to the Promised Land began with the work that God first did in one man, Moses.

Year after year the Midianites were terrorizing the tribes of Israel until God changed Gideon. In the beginning Gideon did not see himself as a leader. He protested that he was the least of his family, that his family was the least in his tribe, and his tribe the least in all of Israel. It was only after God was able to change Gideon's low view of God and himself that He finally convinced Gideon that he was part of the answer to his own prayer of deliverance. Once God worked

in the life of Gideon, the children of Israel were able to over-
come their nemesis.

Esther, at another time in the history of Israel, was
challenged by her uncle to go before her husband, the
king, and speak on behalf of the tribes of Israel. Her uncle,
Mordecai, helped her see that the sovereign God had used
everything that had happened up to that time in her life to
put her in a unique position of influence—at just the right
season—to provide deliverance for her people. Once Esther
caught God's vision for her life, the tribes of Israel realized
theirs.

Most great movements and major victories begin with
a stirring in just one heart and small victories in just one
life. That is why self-leadership is so important. Leaders will
never reach their full potential to impact the tribes around
them until they learn to allow God to lead in the small areas
of their own lives. This is why the first area of focus for a
tribal church leader is on himself and his self-leadership.

The Ten Commitments

Much of what I have learned about self-leadership,
I began learning in earnest many years ago when I participated in a mentoring experience led by Bob Shank called
"The Master's Program."[1] I was part of a group that met for
three years, four times a year, for a one-day intensive. In
these meetings Bob focused our attention on the need for
consistent growth in ten critical areas of life.

1. Spiritual fitness
2. Intellectual fitness
3. Relational fitness[2]
4. Physical fitness
5. Parenting (if applicable)
6. Marriage (if applicable)
7. Personal finances
8. Career success
9. Discipleship of others
10. Personal evangelism

We were challenged over the three-year journey to assess our current reality in light of God's Word and to make specific, incremental changes, or create holy habits, that would move us toward Christ's ideal.

Many times we overestimate what we can change in a short period of time and underestimate what we could accomplish applying right habits over the long haul. In looking at the ten realms of self-leadership listed earlier, the key question becomes: To what single area might you give special attention in the next three-to-four months and what specific holy habit might you adopt that would make personal growth more likely?

We all have flaws that need to be addressed, areas in which we need to give God full reign to grow us. David wrote in Psalm 139:23–24, "Search me, God, and know my heart; test me and know my concerns. See if there is any offensive way in me; and lead me in the everlasting way." David's prayer should be our prayer.

Spiritual Fitness

What does spiritual fitness look like? In John 15:8, Jesus said it is the Father's desire that we "produce much fruit" and so prove to be His disciples. The word *fruit* in the Bible is used in a couple of ways. First, "fruit" is used to describe the very character of Christ. See the "fruit of the spirit" in Galatians 5:23–24, where nine colors of character paint a portrait of Jesus. Fruit bearing is the result of an ongoing, organic process. The nine attributes of love, joy, peace, patience, kindness, goodness, faithfulness, gentleness, and self-control are the true marks of Christian maturity. Luke 6:43–44 states, "A good tree doesn't produce bad fruit; on the other hand, a bad tree doesn't produce good fruit. For each tree is known by its own fruit." So any good fruit produced in a true believer's life comes as a result of a changed nature.

The second way in which "fruit" is used is to describe both physical and spiritual reproduction (see Gen. 9:1, Rom. 1:13, and 1 Cor. 16:15). A believer is fruitful not simply when Christ's character is visible, but also when Christ's mission is accomplished. Spiritual fitness is thus about being formed into the "likeness of Christ." Then, as we live in such a way that Christ is incarnated in our daily lives, "He is lifted up," and others are drawn into a relationship with Him.

So, two simple questions get to the heart of spiritual fitness:

1. Am I more like the person of Jesus today than I was one year ago?

2. As a result of the answer to question No. 1, are those in my sphere of influence coming to know Christ as Lord and Savior?

Those brave enough to do so might ask themselves "How would those closest to me answer these questions about me?"

Intellectual Fitness

Leaders are learners. They are always seeking to grow, to sharpen their skills, and to expand their knowledge. Sometimes this takes the form of the continuation of a formal education. However, more often than not, it is about gaining knowledge through exposure to key people, other ministries, and reading.

I have heard Bill Hybels say many times, when asked about his advice to leaders who want to get better at leading: "Lead something, anything, get around people who are better leaders than you are and read books on leadership." As a result of the Master's Program, I made a commitment to read at least forty books a year on a variety of subjects, including, but not limited to, theology, marriage and family, leadership, and history. This commitment has yielded a rich reservoir from which I can draw in leading the multiple tribes for which I am responsible.

Learning leaders, when around other leaders, do more listening than talking, always asking strategic questions. The answers to these questions help them do a better job of leading their own tribes.

Relational Fitness

All church tribe leaders need close Christian friends. Proverbs 27:17 says, "Iron sharpens iron, and one man sharpens another." In Ecclesiastes 4:9 the writer reminds us, "Two are better than one because they have a good reward for their efforts."

For some reason this seems to be, as a rule, a greater deficiency in male leaders than in female leaders. Perhaps this is because our culture, at least in America, highly regards independence and self-reliance. Perhaps what keeps us from this healthy interdependence is our pride or a desire for secrecy to hide our besetting sins.

The truth is that we all have blind spots, which, if left unaddressed, will, at best, limit our effectiveness as leaders and, at worst, potentially shipwreck our lives and cause us to become disqualified. As Christian leaders, we are always talking to others about the importance of community and accountability. Do we believe in the biblical concepts enough to model them in our own lives? Two questions:

1. Are you currently in a small group of believers where you are not the leader or supervising the other participants?
2. Are there one or two (same-gender) individuals with whom you meet on a regular basis, who know your strengths, weaknesses, besetting sins, and tendencies, and who currently have permission to ask you the tough questions, and if necessary, be rude to you for Christ's sake?

Physical Fitness

This one is harder to fake. I can pretend to be spiritually, intellectually, and relationally fit, but when I step on the scales, the numbers do not lie. Yes, this body—this temporary tent—is going to be put in the ground one day and return to dust. But until that glorious day, it is the vehicle in which we dwell as we lead our tribe. If we do not get adequate exercise, eat the right fuel, and get enough sleep, we handicap our effectiveness as leaders in at least two ways.

First, we limit the amount of energy available for the energy-demanding role of a tribal leader. For more on this, I recommend *The Power of Full Engagement*, by Jim Loehr and Tony Schwartz.[3] The authors argue that managing energy—not time—is the key to high performance and personal renewal.

Second, when it becomes obvious to others that we are being poor stewards of our bodies, this hurts our credibility with those in the tribes we lead.

Parenting

According to the apostle Paul, one prerequisite for leadership in the church is effective leadership in one's own home tribe. He writes, "If anyone does not know how to manage his own household, how will he take care of God's church?" (1 Tim. 3:5).

It is sad that in an effort to win the world, we can lose our own family in the process. Years ago when Lake Pointe was a very young church, I fell into a dangerous pattern of "drivenness" in order to reach our community for Christ. As a result, my schedule evolved to the point that I was home only one night a week.

One Sunday I was having a hallway discussion with the wife of a prominent minister who was our guest speaker for the day. When I asked about their children, she informed me that their children did not have a close relationship with their dad because he had neglected them in their formative years in order to build a "great church." On one hand, this was way too much information; on the other, it was just what I needed to hear.

That day was a defining moment for my family and me. I decided to reverse my daily calendar and seek to be gone from home no more than one night a week. I accepted the fact that the growth of our church would, by necessity, be curtailed. I think it is rather ironic that when you look back statistically over the years, it was during the following year that our church began to grow numerically at a more substantial pace than ever before. As I chose to make my family relationships the priority, God blessed our fellowship in a way that no amount of effort on my part could have created.

Marriage

Leaders must give priority to their priority relationships. If you are married, your relationship with your spouse is the highest in the human hierarchy. The title of John O'Neil's book, *The Paradox of Success: When Winning at Work Means Losing at Life*,[4] is an apt, yet unfortunate, description of some leaders' home lives. It can happen before we fully know it. The rewards of achieving at the office can be more immediate and tangible than those at home. The intimacy that marriage creates engenders conflict. Conflict is a part of God's design so that we can choose to love and give away our selfishness to become more other-centered. However, because we are creatures who crave comfort, there is always the temptation to avoid such character-testing intimacy.

We enter marriage with many self-centered expectations. These expectations are then hammered with the daily realities of seemingly incongruent personalities, differing childhood models of family, idiosyncrasies, annoying habits, and the downright sinfulness of the two individuals joined together, all of which are intensified by sharing a checkbook, bathroom, and bed. The gap between our expectations and our reality is what I call the "disappointment gap." You can replace the word *disappointment* with "anger," "frustration," "depression," or the emotion of your choice. Many times we expect our spouse to meet needs in our lives that only God can meet. As Christians, we have the promise that God is going to meet all of our needs according to the riches of Christ Jesus. There is no question that He intends to meet some of those needs through our spouse. God, however, is not frustrated by their lack of cooperation.

When we depend solely on our spouses, we are in effect giving them God's job description. A husband or wife, when given the opportunity, can make a pretty good partner. But a spouse makes a terrible god.

Part of the solution is to lower our expectation of the other person and what any human relationship can really provide. The other part is to do the necessary work to raise reality by resolving conflicts, communicating needs, and exercising forgiveness.

Given the effort required to navigate the minefield of marriage, it is easy to see why one might be tempted to spend greater amounts of energy and time in a realm where one is the center of attention and has the authority to fire some, if not all, of the individuals who might have a different point of view.

I married much too young (age nineteen) with way too little knowledge about both the rigors of marriage and the differences between men and women. My wife, Marsha, describes the first three years of her marriage to a strong-willed, verbally gifted communicator—who used those skills to almost always get his way—as a type of "hell." In the thirty-eight years of our marriage, that is the closest I've ever heard her come to uttering anything close to profanity.

So, "Houston, we had a problem." Neither of our theologies permitted an easy way out so we were stuck with each other. Knowing divorce was not an option, we set out to make our relationship work. We read every book on marriage we could get our hands on, sought the counsel of and learned from couples we knew and respected. We both had to learn the uncomfortable but essential skill of "speaking the truth in love" (Eph. 4:15, 25, 29).

Marsha, because of her personality, has had to work on the "speak truth" and "don't let the sun set on your anger" parts. I have had to work on the "love" and "let no unwholesome word depart from your mouth" parts.

While our marriage is still very much a work in progress, after three decades of weekly date nights, mini personal marriage retreats, dreaming together and planning our shared future, and learning how to let go of the past, we have found that the love of Christ has empowered us to become best friends and a team in ministry. (I share more extensively on this topic in my book *It Starts at Home*.[5])

Personal Finances

My earliest memories of childhood are of spending Saturday mornings lying with my brothers on the top of the kitchen table in our trailer house, watching cartoons on the black-and-white television that sat on top of the refrigerator. Other kids had color television sets and comfortable living room recliners. Our family made do with much less. But I had a rich childhood in many other ways, including the instruction I received about money at an early age. I remember when I mowed my first lawn for money. I mowed, edged, raked, and swept the front and back yard for $10 (the price paid should give you an idea of my age). When I arrived home that day, my dad asked me if I knew what I was going to do with my hard-earned cash. I replied that I had a pretty good idea.

Dad then informed me that he was going to take the $10 and exchange it for one five-dollar bill and five one-dollar bills. He then proceeded to instruct me that I was to take the first dollar with me to church the next Sunday and place it in the offering plate. This would be a way to acknowledge "that God had given me the ability to earn that money." The second dollar, he said, was headed to the Trinity Savings and Loan down on Buckner Boulevard, where I was going to open my first savings account. He said, "One of these days you are going to want to own a car. If so, you will need to pay for half of it. And one day you may want to go to college. If so, you will pay for half of that also. So you had better start saving for both."

Thus, I began to live on the 10/10/80 plan. Over the years, I found you can give God at least 10 percent of your income and save at least 10 percent of the money you earn and somehow survive on 80 percent or less. On the other hand, I have learned after many years of counseling others that the 0/0/110 plan does not work. No matter how you figure it, paying someone else interest to use their money in order to buy something today—which you could wait and save to purchase—is a form of immaturity as well as stupidity. I learned that financial mismanagement is not as much a math problem as it is a "willingness to work" problem, or an "I want more than I can afford" problem.

Many of us struggle with how much material stuff is enough. It is not enough to just avoid debt by working hard, paying cash, and avoiding interest by paying off the credit card each month. We must ask the tough questions like, "What does sacrificial giving really look like for an American who has entirely too many clothes and who lives in a house that would be considered a mansion almost anywhere else in the world?" Even if we lived on only 50 percent of our income, we would live better than 90 percent of the world.

These are just some of the issues with which each of us must wrestle in order to model God-honoring stewardship for the tribes we lead.

Career Success

I believe God created everyone to be great at something, and that when people find themselves unfulfilled or unsuccessful in their chosen field, one or more of the following is true:

1. They are in the wrong profession.
2. They are in the wrong role in the right profession.
3. They are working with or for the wrong people. (Most people do not quit their jobs; they quit their bosses.)
4. They are working for the wrong reason(s). (This causes people to work too many hours and many times in the wrong profession.)
5. They do not have a proper, biblical theology of work.[6]

All of us spend way too many hours working every week to be doing something we do not enjoy and in which we cannot excel. There are many reasons why people go to work at a particular place and in a particular role, many of which make no sense at all.

In seeking to find the right role, we need to consider how God has uniquely created us, how our life experiences have shaped us, and what we are passionate about. The answers to these questions provide clues to finding greater fulfillment and productivity in our work. There are some great resources available today to help us discover the role in which we will be most productive and fulfilled. I have found that even those in the right role in the right job can benefit from these tools to refine their job description.

1. *StrengthsFinder 2.0* by Tom Rath. This volume includes a code that allows you to access and take a twenty-minute online inventory that will reveal your top five strengths, in order, out of a possible thirty-four strengths. This is

not a personality inventory. It provides a totally different measurement and, when combined with a personality inventory, will give tremendous insight to determine a perfect fit.[7]

2. *Leading from Your Strengths* online inventory. This is a refined form of the D.I.S.C. personality inventory, which will provide a twenty-eight-page report. The report helps you understand how you respond to change, pace, and problem solving and whether you are task-oriented or relationally-oriented. Go to ministryinsights.com.[8]

3. Any good online Spiritual Gifts Profile.[9]

In ministry, many times we are guilty of mimicking other ministries instead of creating our own unique expression of who we are and the particular tribes we are called to reach. At a conference I attended years ago, I heard Leonard Sweet say that during the 1980s many young pastors tried to re-create the ministry of Bill Hybels at Willow Creek in their own communities and that many of them, in the words of Leonard Sweet, "found themselves up a Willow Creek without a Hybels."

I have found it is also insightful to examine the activities we perform each day and make sure they are in alignment with our abilities. Everything we attempt to do will fall into one of the following four categories:

1. Activities we do not do well.
2. Tasks at which we are average.
3. Things we do really well.

4. Those activities at which we are better than almost everyone. Some would say these things fit our "unique competency."

For obvious reasons we should all strive to do less of those activities that we do not do well and tasks at which we are only average. I also recommend even decreasing the time we spend doing things we do well. The time saved can be invested in those endeavors that fit in our unique strength area. Many times the difference between activities that flow out of our unique strength and those things we do well are indistinguishable to the outside observer. We, however, know that our unique ability activities are those that energize us rather than deplete us. This is the primary reason tribal leaders should seek, whenever possible, to delegate or "outsource" all tasks other than those that fit his or her unique ability.

One of the most common questions I receive about hiring staff is, "What position should I hire next?" That obviously will vary from church to church. However, in most cases, I have found that pastor-level leaders do not have adequate administrative help. Consequently many ministers find themselves doing administrative tasks that could be delegated to someone else so that they can better leverage their own time and abilities. Almost every time you can hire someone in a lower pay grade or recruit a volunteer in order to give away tasks currently being done by a person in a higher pay grade, you increase productivity and expand ministry effectiveness.

I also believe it is important to schedule your most essential tasks during the time of the day when you are at your best. Most of us operate better at a particular time of day. For some, the most creative and energetic time is in the morning. For others, afternoon brings a second wind. Still others thrive during the evening hours.

Mornings are best for me. As a result, I reserve large blocks of time early in the day for sermon preparation, strategic planning, and important leadership meetings. My afternoons are made available for less-strategic meetings that impact fewer people, such as counseling or responding to the requests of others. I also get a second burst of energy at night, and this is why I try to be home most evenings. My family deserves some of my most creative and energetic times.

Discipleship of Others

Every one of us needs both a Paul and a Timothy in our life. We all need to be coaching and mentoring someone new to the faith, and we all need to be the object of some form of coaching and mentoring.

As a minister, I find seasons of my life when I am not discipling anyone except my direct reports as a part of my job as the leader of my church. Over the years I have been convicted that it is both my responsibility and my privilege to disciple others as a non-professional, individual Christian. One of the most refreshing joys and edifying moments we can experience as believers is to pray for, witness to, and invite someone until they become followers of Christ. Then once they place their faith in Christ, we should help them learn how to study the Bible, memorize Scripture, pray to God, resist temptation, worship, witness to others, and by His grace, become more like Christ.

As leaders, we touch the lives of others in multiple ways as we lead those who minister to others. But we should never become so busy or so isolated that we fail to directly impact the lives of those whom God has put in our own personal sphere of influence.

Personal Evangelism

A disclaimer may be appropriate here. In addition to the spiritual gifts of leadership and teaching, God's spirit has graced me with the gift of evangelism. On the day God saved me, He gave me the supernatural ability and the accompanying passion to lead people to Christ. This means, among other things, that I can smell a lost person from across the room, and shortly after meeting him or her, I am able to determine where that person is on his or her journey toward God. I can also quickly, and in a non-offensive manner, ascertain whether the individual has any desire to move closer to Him and what the next step could be in that process. All of this has nothing to do with my effort. It is a gift—just like your own spiritual gift(s).

This gifting also makes me quite passionate to see the whole body of Christ mobilized to share His love with a lost and dying world. Please do not write off my encouragement to you as gift projection on my part. While I realize that not all of us have the specific spiritual gift of evangelism, all of us are commanded to be witnesses.

In fact, Jesus said prior to His ascension that all of us would be witnesses (Acts 1:8). The only question that remains is whether or not we will be faithful and effective witnesses. Are we moving people toward Christ or driving them away from Christ?

The Bible says that there is a gift of giving, a special supernatural ability to make money and wisely invest it in God's kingdom (Rom. 12:8). Yet, all of us, even without that specific gift, are commanded to give (2 Cor. 9:7).

There is the spiritual gift of faith, the supernatural ability to believe God for great things (1 Cor. 12:9). Yet the Bible tells all of us in Hebrews that without faith it is impossible to please God. In the same way, some of us are uniquely gifted to share our faith, but all of us are to be participants in evangelism.

Sometimes I think that those of us who have the gift of evangelism expect everyone to share Christ in the same style in which we are comfortable sharing. We tell stories about witnessing to a total stranger on a three-hour plane ride from Chicago to Dallas, and our people think, "Well, I could never do that." As a result of rejecting our style, intensity, or method, they exclude themselves from the entire process.

Paul tells us that one believer plants the seed, another waters, and God gives the increase (1 Cor. 3:6–8). More of our people would serve on the team to evangelize if they could come to understand that their participation is just a part of the process and that they do not always have to be the one who "closes the sale."

In order for them to understand that witnessing is as natural as recommending a great restaurant or a good movie—things we do all the time—they need to understand that witnessing—most of the time—is more of a sentence than a paragraph. Witnessing does not require them to be biblical scholars or to be able to answer every question asked, but rather they only have to share the biblical truth that they have personally experienced.

Conclusion

We cannot expect those in our tribe to tend to the ten realms of self-leadership if we are not living it ourselves and are not open to the new and fresh winds of the Spirit blowing in our own lives. I like the way Paul the apostle describes self-leadership in 1 Corinthians 9:24–27:

> Do you not know that the runners in a stadium all race, but only one receives the prize? Run in such a way that you may win. Now everyone who competes exercises self-control in everything. However, they do it to receive a perishable crown, but we an imperishable. Therefore I do not run like one who runs aimlessly, or box like one who beats the air. Instead I discipline my body and bring it under strict control, so that after preaching to others, I myself will not be disqualified.

Before he could lead anyone else, Paul knew he had to exercise—by God's grace—self-leadership. May his tribe increase.

Leading Small Action Plans

Get started applying the concepts explored in this chapter to your life by reflecting on the following questions.

Self and Family Leadership

On a scale of 1 to 10, how would you rate your level of intentionality in each of the following areas over the past 120 days?

- Spiritual fitness: Becoming more like Jesus through spiritual disciplines
- Intellectual fitness: Listening and reading to learn from others
- Relational fitness: Inviting same-gender friends to speak into my life
- Physical fitness: Stewardship of my body
- Parenting: Investing in the faith of my own children at home
- Marriage: Loving and serving my spouse
- Personal finances: Living within my income, while saving 10 percent and giving 10 percent or more
- Career success: Leveraging my unique strengths
- Discipleship of others: Investing myself into new believers and young leaders
- Personal evangelism: Sharing Christ with others

Which area needs an inordinate amount of attention during the next 120 days to help you become a more effective leader?

What specific discipline will you start? How often? What days? What time? Who will hold you accountable?

To make it easy to go deeper on the themes of this chapter we have provided a free video overview. Invite your leaders to watch the corresponding segment and come to the next team meeting ready to discuss the "Leading Small Action Plan" questions. Access the video at: TribalChurchBook.com.

Chapter Two

Leading Your Own Tribe

Church leaders long to make a significant impact with their ministries like so many have before them. Yet many overlook one of the most critical requirements of church leadership, one that was imbedded in the DNA of the Christ movement from the beginning. As the first Christian churches were being planted, in a letter written to a young leader, the apostle Paul said that if a man does not manage his own household (tribe) well, then he has no business leading the church (1 Tim. 3:5).

We must be true to this biblical mandate for the benefit of our own families, as well as for the other tribes of families we lead. As Christian leaders, it is vital that we model what we teach. Perfection is not the issue or we would all be disqualified. Instead, there should be a reasonable alignment between what we teach about family life and what we practice. The problem is that the very demands of leading a church can sometimes compete with our vital incarnational leadership at home.

What does it mean to lead your own family? Let us begin by giving a general definition of a leader. What is the irreducible core that clarifies what leadership is all about? Put simply: *a leader is someone who leads*.

I have shared this "profound" definition around the world in places like Africa, Egypt, China, Australia, Russia, and many other places. The response is always the same; people are left speechless—overwhelmed by such a razor-sharp insight.

But, really, it is true.

- Leadership is not a title. It is not a position.
- A leader is someone who gets out front and sets the direction for others.
- A leader anticipates and solves problems before anybody else knows that there are problems.
- Leaders inspire.
- Leaders encourage.
- Leaders coach.
- Leaders counsel.
- Put simply, leaders go first.

And the most important "proving ground" for leaders is their immediate and most important tribe—their family. What does any leader do in his or her home? What does it mean to lead one's own tribe? What does that look like when it happens? There are three essential keys to effective leadership in one's own home.

Leaders Clarify Purpose

First, leading at home means clarifying purpose and casting vision. To cast a vision means painting a picture for a preferred future based upon God's intended design for the home. The vision is ever-evolving as a current expression of a never-changing purpose. The purpose remains constant, answering the question: "What does God want us to be and do as a family?"

Purpose-aligned vision casting is the first thing a church leader is also called to do for a church. Fortunately we do not have to manufacture a purpose for the church. God has already revealed in Matthew 28:19–20 that the purpose of the church is to make disciples.

At Lake Pointe we express it this way: God has called us as a church to *Share Christ and Build Believers.*

Now the good news is that just as God has given us a purpose for the church, He has also provided a clear answer to the question, "What is the purpose of the family?" In Deuteronomy 6:4–5 it says this:

> "Listen, Israel: The LORD is our God, the
> LORD is One. Love the LORD your God with all
> your heart, with all your soul, and with all your
> strength."

These two verses comprise what is known as the *Shema*, a short summary that the Jewish people repeated twice a day, every day, to remind their family of their primary purpose.

These words were first uttered by Moses after the children of Israel had spent forty years in the wilderness. Moses made this declaration as he was about to hand the baton of leadership over to Joshua, just before the nation of Israel entered the Promised Land. These words reflected critical instructions to the people of God as they entered a new season as a nation of tribes.

Let me remind you that Moses delivered this message from God to the twelve tribes of Israel. What is a tribe? A tribe is a family. So the words of the *Shema* were first uttered by Moses, the leader of the children of Israel, to remind those tribes or families who were transitioning from the wilderness experience into the prosperity of the Promised Land. His message was simple, but significant: "Never forget that you are to model and teach your family what it means to love God."

Why the reminder? I am convinced that remembering the purpose of the family was actually easier in the wilderness where they were constantly reminded of God's provision and presence. Each day a cloud of smoke visibly led the way they were to go. Every night before they went to sleep, they could look out of their tent and see a pillar of fire representing the faithful presence of God. Every morning when they got up they found manna that God had placed on the ground for breakfast, a repeated reminder that their very existence depended upon God's provision. They did not need verbal reminders that without God they might end up both lost and hungry. Those reminders surrounded them every single day.

But things were about to change. They were about to experience the plush lifestyle that was to be afforded by the Promised Land. In the Promised Land they would perhaps no longer live lives desperate for God because of their constant needs. Instead, they would live lives distracted from God because their most pressing needs would be met. Their prosperity could blind them to the fact that it was God who had brought them to that amazing place.

We, too, need to hear and obey the *Shema* today. Our purpose as families is easily forgotten in the busyness of life. While preparing to go to college, launching a new career, buying that first car, decorating our first home, or planning our next vacation, our focus on God can get fuzzy. Moses' words are a needed challenge to all of us. They are a good reminder to young parents who want so much for their children to enjoy a high standard of living, to parents who are paying hard-earned money to coaches and tutors, and to parents who spend countless hours taking their kids to lessons so that they can dance better, hit the ball farther, or achieve greater academic success. Moses reminds us with the *Shema*, "It is great for your children to have things and to be rich in experiences, but do not let them be poor in their relationship with God."

Moses reminds us that loving God should be the central purpose of every family. Above all else, it is your own relationship and your family's relationship with God that matter most.

As recorded in Exodus 20:3–6, Moses stressed a similar principle amid the giving of the Ten Commandments.

> Do not have other gods besides Me.
> Do not make an idol for yourself, whether in the shape of anything in the heavens above or on the earth below or in the waters under the earth.
> You must not bow down to them or worship them; for I, the LORD your God, am a jealous

> God, punishing the children for the fathers' sin
> to the third and fourth generations of those who
> hate Me, but showing faithful love to a thousand
> generations of those who love Me and keep My
> commands.

Families who love God reap the blessings of that love for generations, while the descendants of those who hate God suffer the consequences.

What the *Shema* is also emphasizing is how we miss the point whenever we allow our faith to become just a set of rules. This vision is about so much more than making sure we raise well-behaved boys and girls. If we only hand down the rules that God has given without the corresponding relationship into which God invites us, we risk passing on an empty, lifeless religion. Compliance to an external standard or attempting to obey a set of rules will not inspire a love relationship or an internal passion.

When I was young, I would often ask my parents "Why?" when they told me to do something I did not want to do. Mom and Dad gave the same response time and time again. They would say, "Because I told you to." I recall thinking to myself at the time, *When I am an adult, I am going to be a better parent than my mom and dad. When my kids ask "Why?" I will explain my reasons.*

When my two girls were old enough they, like their father had done, frequently asked the "why" question. So I sat down and explained my entire rationale to them concerning whatever request or demand I was making. The impact was remarkable! They looked up at me with admiration in their eyes and said, "Oh, Father, thou art so wise." After which they immediately obeyed with a wonderful spirit of submission and joy (pause here for incredulous doubt or raucous laughter).

In truth, they were not impressed with my explanations in the least. I very quickly learned that the best response when they questioned my orders was to say "You will obey me because I am your dad and because I have lived longer than you, and I am trying to pass down to you what God has told me and what God has taught me. I do not want you to make some of the mistakes that I made. You will have to do it just because you trust me, because you respect my role as your parent."

In other words, "Because I told you to."

Guiding our children is all about respect, rooted in a relationship. I did not train my children to obey any command from just any person. That would be foolish. I raised them to trust my instructions because of their relationship with me.

There are not enough restraints, force, money, or private detectives in the world to ensure our kids do what we want them to do. Their compliance to our values must be based on a relationship. As children grow up, the only true leverage a parent has is rooted in the fact that you have modeled a love that inspires and nurtures your child's trust.

Moses understood that the key to obedience is the belief that God can be trusted. That is why his emphasis is on the lawgiver more than the law. We may not always understand why God gives certain commandments or restrictions. We may not always understand why God encourages us to take

risks in the way that He asks us to take risks. But we can
trust Him. Basically, Moses said to the tribes, "God has
been faithful for forty years. He has brought us to this place.
He has kept His promises in spite of our hardheartedness.
Remember that, and love God. Choose to love God with all
of your intellect, with all of your emotions, and even with
all of your physical might. As a three-dimensional person,
love God completely. Remember that loving God is our main
business of life. Remember it when you go into His new land,
and pass this central truth on to your family and to each succeeding generation of families."

Every year family members struggle over what to give
Dad for Father's Day. After all, in most homes, Dad has the
largest earning power. He pretty much has all of the things
that he wants, or if not, he could go out and get them at any
time for himself. So what in the world does a five-year-old
kid give to Dad for Father's Day, a birthday, or Christmas? In
a word: obedience.

What do you give to a God who has created everything?
God says, "If you love Me, keep My commandments." What
does it mean to keep His commandments? It is not about
striving or straining to be good enough. It is about trusting
His heart enough to submit to His guidance.

Most of us grew up talking about "faith" in God.
Sometimes we use the word to the point that it becomes
stale. For some reason we identify "faith" with some kind
of emotional feeling we attempt to conjure up. But faith
is actually a synonym for trust. If God has been trustworthy, then trust Him. The way we demonstrate that trust
is through obedience.

When I was a child, our church sang an old hymn with these words: "Trust and obey for there's no other way to be happy in Jesus, but to trust and obey." The older I get, the more I realize the futility of efforts to try harder to be good, motivated by fear, guilt, or even shame. The best gift I can give to God and the best model I can provide for my family is the gift of trusting God out of love.

As the leaders of our homes, we must clarify what it really means to be a great family. Great families show love for God by trusting God.

Leaders Implement an Effective Strategy

A leader of a family first clarifies purpose and casts vision. The second key to effective family leadership is implementing an effective strategy. In Deuteronomy 6:7–9, Moses offers a clear and specific plan for effective families. The words are quite familiar to most of us:

> Repeat them to your children. Talk about them
> when you sit in your house and when you walk
> along the road, when you lie down and when you
> get up. Bind them as a sign on your hand and let
> them be a symbol on your forehead. Write them
> on the doorposts of your house and on your gates.

Moses offers very specific, practical strategies for inspiring faith in the next generation. We are to do it: (1) *As you sit*. For most of us, that is mealtime. (2) *As you walk along the road*. That is travel time. We do not walk much these days. But most families do a great deal of driving together. (3) *As you lie down*. On most days, we finally get around to doing that, do we not? Although we may do it at different times, Moses is describing bedtime. (4) *When you get up*. The first thing each morning, we are to begin our day pointing our tribe to God.

Moses is not asking families to add a bunch of new activities to an already over-crowded schedule. Every day we already sit down at the table. Every day we travel somewhere. Every day we go to bed, and every morning we get up. We are to use the rhythms already built into life rather than trying to create artificial occasions for spiritually vital conversations.

One of the things I love about this plan is its **efficiency**. This plan leverages one activity for multiple purposes. What does that look like? Let us say you have not had time to exercise because you are trying to spend more time with the kids. Being efficient says you get exercise by playing tennis *with* your kids. This plan says have spiritual conversations and experiences with your children in the time frames that already exist!

Another component to this strategy is **longevity**. I believe we almost always overestimate what we can do in a short amount of time. We cannot neglect our families all year long and think going to Disney World for four days will make up for it. We also underestimate what we can do over the long haul if we keep after it, and we continue doing it, and if we stay consistent. If you do not believe that, look at the Grand Canyon. The greatest work you will ever do in your family will occur each day at the breakfast table and each night while tucking the kids into bed. Little by little. That is consistency.

This plan that God has given us also utilizes **repetition**. Why is it that you cannot remember your driver's license number, but you can remember a song that you first heard when you were in middle school? (In my case the Beach Boys' "In my Room" or the Beatles' "I Wanna Hold Your Hand.") Repetition. There is a certain rhythm to music that makes you want to sing it over and over again. The repetition imbeds it into your memory and brands it into your heart. In the same way, Moses calls us to attach our central purpose as a family into the natural rhythm of life.

The Jewish home had that kind of rhythm. They repeated the *Shema* twice a day. They also talked about God when they got up each day, when they ate, when they traveled, and when they went to bed. They had a rhythm to their day. They also had a rhythm to their week. They called it the Sabbath. They were highly intentional about making one day per week different than every other day. It became a symbol of their trust in God.

The Sabbath was highly countercultural and risky because stopping their labor as a family meant they would have to depend on God to provide for their needs. Every day of the week, they would reflect on God's purpose for their family and share it with their children throughout the regular activities of each day. But one day a week they would pause and give an inordinate amount of attention to intense reflection, worship, and their expression of trust in God. Most church leaders do a poor job of keeping the Sabbath.

(If you struggle with keeping the Sabbath in your own life, I suggest reading Mark Buchanan's book, *The Rest of God.* [1])

They also had annual rhythms including regular festivals and feasts, such as the celebration of Passover, that became catalytic reminders of what life was really all about for them and their families (see Lev. 23:4–7).

We have the same kind of opportunities today. Although we may not celebrate the Jewish feasts and festivals, our families do experience cycles and events that can be used for similar purposes. These recurring celebrations can serve as routine reminders and as a part of our strategy to help our tribe think about the priority of relationship and obedience to God. We can leverage occasions such as Christmas, Thanksgiving, Easter, and other holidays that already have a clear connection to our Christian belief.

We can also use less obvious holidays like Father's Day to trigger a discussion with our families about our Father in heaven. We can remind our tribe that all earthly fathers have some level of imperfection or even dysfunction. But there is a heavenly Father who is perfect, and we should talk about that as a family on Father's Day. It is important to remember the characteristics of our heavenly Father, which every earthly father should try to emulate, reminding his family that He is trustworthy.

Another celebration opportunity is the date of each family member's spiritual birthday. Every time I have the privilege to lead a young person to Christ, I tell that young man or woman to open up his or her Bible and record the date. If the child is younger, I turn to the parent and say, "This is a special day. You need to celebrate this day every year with your child." I then turn to the child and say, "Every year on this day, you get to pick your favorite restaurant. (Easy for me to say that since I am not paying!) You do not get any presents, but you get to pick where to eat. When you go to your favorite restaurant, you can talk about what happened today and the promises that you made to God today. When that day comes every year, talk about the difference that God has made and is still making in your life."

Like the Jewish people, we can leverage the annual rhythms and events of our lives as a part of our strategy to reinforce the purpose of the family. As family leaders, we must see to it that God's strategy is implemented in our tribe. We must use the activities and events that are already a part of the fabric of our daily, weekly, and annual life, and leverage them to remind our family of our God-honoring purpose.[2]

Leaders Live the Vision

The third and most important key to leading in our home is that we embody or live out the vision. In Moses' words, "These words, that I am giving you today are to be in *your heart*" (Deut. 6:6, emphasis mine). Tribal leaders can only effectively transfer what they themselves possess.

What is not happening in your tribe, in your family, that you wish was happening? As a leader in your tribe, you must *lead out* in that virtue or value. If you want your family to be more generous, then you must first be more generous. If you want the people in your home to be more patient, then you need to be the one who models patience. If you want more sensitivity, if you want more kindness, if you want more romance—model them all.

A leader lives and embodies the vision so that over time the culture of the tribe is established. That is what great leaders do! All of us, to some extent, are visual learners. We really do not fully "get it" until we see it lived out. Our families will best understand the vision when they see it lived out in our lives.

In 1 Corinthians 11:1, Paul wrote: "Be imitators of me, as I also am of Christ." How many of us can—or would want to—say this to our own children:

- "Hey, kids, live your lives like I am living mine."
- "I want you to handle your money like I handle mine."
- "I want you to cherish your future wife like I cherish your mommy."
- "I want you to think the thoughts that I am thinking.
- I want you to watch the movies that I am watching.
- I want you to treat the poor like I am treating the poor.
- I want you to trust God like I am trusting God."

This is what it really means to lead and not just talk a big game or tell others what they should be doing.

Leading is more than strategizing.

Leading is more than creating a plan.

Leading is also about becoming a living picture of the vision!

When Jesus was asked, "What is the greatest commandment?", He responded by quoting the *Shema* from Deuteronomy 6 about how we are to love God. But then

He added these words, "The second is: Love your neighbor as yourself. There is no commandment greater than these" (Mark 12:31). Why did Jesus add to the *Shema*? Was Christ watering down the fact that the purpose of our lives—the purpose of our family—is to love God? Quite the opposite. He was clarifying *how* to love God. We love God by loving others.

Earlier we noted that we love God by trusting Him enough to keep His commandments. What key commandment does He give us to obey other than to love Him? It is to love others.

In 1 John 4:20, the apostle wrote, "If anyone says, 'I love God,' yet hates his brother, he is a liar. For the person who does not love his brother whom he has seen cannot love God whom he has not seen." If you say you love God and you hate your wife, you are a liar. If you say you love God and you hate your husband, you are a liar. If you say you love God and you hate your brother, you are blowing smoke.

The best way I can lead my family is to love my family. And one of the ways I demonstrate my love is when we sit down together at mealtime and ask, "Hey, what is going on in your life that I need to know about? How can I pray for you?"

I demonstrate my love when we are traveling by turning off the radio or DVD player to talk about the kind of family we want to be. I demonstrate my love by taking time to dream together with my family about what we could be for God's glory.

I demonstrate my love when I read stories to my children rather than barking the order for them to go to bed. I love my family by telling them about God's faithfulness in my own life.

I demonstrate my love when I get up in the morning and cast a vision for each family member about them loving someone today who is not in our family, someone who God loves, but who no one else in this world loves. I demonstrate my love to my family by praying that God will put someone in their path, today, someone who needs something that they have. The vision I cast is: "Hey, today you will have an opportunity to choose between the dark side and God's side, and what will you choose?"

I love my family by giving, by serving, by sharing, by listening, and by forgiving.

Little by little. Day by day. When I sit down; when I walk by the way; when I go to sleep at night, and when I rise each new morning.

There is no more important place to lead than in your home. What is the purpose of the family? To love God, to love each other, and then as a family, to love others. It is all about relationships. And when we get to the end of time, nothing else is going to matter.

Before we can effectively lead the tribes at church, we must first lead the tribe God has given us at home. We must lead our family to love God, and we must love our family to lead them.

Leading Small Action Plans

Get started applying the concepts explored in this chapter to your life by honestly assessing how intentional you have been at home. Which of the following have you done (or not done) over the past 120 days?

Marriage Intentionality

Check all that apply.

- ❑ I had a "date night" twice or more per month to focus on one another without the children.
- ❑ I wrote a note, gave a flower or some other tangible expression of love at least twice per month.
- ❑ I called during the day, sat down to chat, took walks together, or took some other time of focused, non-task-driven communication at least three times per week.
- ❑ I prayed with my spouse (other than saying grace over a meal) at least twice per week.
- ❑ I demonstrated meaningful touch (hugs, kisses, caressing) and/or verbal affirmation (words of appreciation, admiration, affection) at least once per day.
- ❑ I took steps to reduce risk to my marriage in vulnerable areas (bad temper, sexual temptation, office relationships, time away from home, demeaning language, substance abuse, etc.) by establishing and/or maintaining boundaries, increasing accountability, etc.
- ❑ I made a consistent effort to take care of myself physically and emotionally to be the best lifelong partner I can be.

❏ I admitted I was wrong and apologized and/or forgave *before going to bed* after conflicts with my spouse.

Parental Intentionality

Check all that apply.

❏ I did something special with my children (hobby, ice cream date, movie night, etc.) at least twice per month.

❏ I connected relationally with my children (chatting, helping with homework, eating dinner together at the table, etc.) at least once per day.

❏ I created or captured an occasion within the home for passing my beliefs and values to my children (family night activity, mealtime conversation, bedtime reading, etc.) at least once per week.

❏ I prayed with my children (including meals, bedtime, etc.) at least five times per week.

❏ I participated in some type of intergenerational faith experience in addition to regular worship services (a service project, family mission trip, volunteer in children's ministry, father/daughter banquet, father/son event, etc.) at least once in the past four months.

To make it easy to go deeper on the themes of this chapter we have provided a free video overview. Invite your leaders to watch the corresponding segment and come to the next team meeting ready to discuss the "Leading Small Action Plan" questions. Access the video at: TribalChurchBook.com.

Chapter Three
The First Tribe

As we discuss how to become a tribal church, we must begin with the single most important strategic priority for any tribal leader: helping your people create God-honoring homes. Long before God created the church, God created the original tribe, the family. Scripture tells us that God formed man out of the dust of the ground, breathed into his nostrils the breath of life, and man became a living soul. The Bible then recounts that God saw the man was alone and for the first time declared something He created "not good." That does not mean it was bad, but that it was incomplete. We were not created to live in isolation. We were made to live in communion with others. So God created the first tribe, the family.

God caused the first man to fall into a deep sleep, took a rib from his side, and created woman. When the man woke from his God-induced sleep and saw his mate beside him, he declared, "bone of my bone, flesh of my flesh." I am convinced he could have continued with "member of my tribe" as well because the concept of tribe is as foundational to our

God-given design and purpose as the very image of triune God.

Lake Pointe Values

Over the past thirty-two years, thirteen values have guided our strategic efforts, one of which speaks to the critical role of the family (see Value 12).

1. Lost people matter.
2. All Christians should be fully-developing followers of Jesus Christ.
3. The church can worship God in a seeker-sensitive manner.
4. The church should be culturally relevant while remaining doctrinally pure.
5. Every aspect of the church should be purpose-driven.
6. The church ought to be a positive contributing member of both the local and global community.
7. Strategic systems help the church accomplish its goals.
8. God's work deserves our best.
9. Individuals serve most effectively on teams.
10. Life change happens best in purpose-driven small groups.
11. All relationships should be marked by truth telling and love.
12. God designed the family to be the primary disciple-making relationship.
13. Strategic development and mentoring of emerging leaders is essential to healthy church growth.

These thirteen values have served as a guiding strategy of our ministry. From the very beginning, we affirmed Value 12, that *the family is God's primary vehicle for spiritual formation*. This particular value has always been especially important to me because I had the great blessing of growing up in a family where my parents made the family tribe a top priority. As the senior leader of Lake Pointe, I want the same life-changing experience for all of the people of our church.

But, this particular value has proven to be among the most difficult to uphold. I recognized this in 2006 when I asked our elders and key staff members to rank how well we, as a church, were living out each of our thirteen core values. Imagine my surprise to discover that the leaders of our church ranked the implementation of Value 12 (family as the primary vehicle for spiritual formation) dead last! The reason was not that we did not believe in the importance and priority of the home. We did. But, for a variety of reasons, we were not effectively turning that belief into reality in our people.

The reasons for this were many, but I'll just mention a couple.

First, we discovered that the parents in our church had a tendency to outsource the responsibility of discipling their own children to the church. They outsourced the discipling of their kids to the church much like they outsource athletics to the coach, education to the school, and music to the piano teacher. They viewed the church as the "expert" for all things spiritual. They thought that Lake Pointe's well-developed Student Ministry team knew more about their teenagers than they did and that a professionally-trained Children's Ministry team knew more about how to form their child's faith than they did.

Even if their assumptions were true, the church could not, of course, do all the necessary work of spiritual formation in the one or two hours that we had their child's attention. The time kids spend at home, at school, and with friends easily dwarfs the access provided to the best youth pastor or Sunday school teacher.

Second, we discovered that we, as the leaders of the church, had failed to clearly declare that the primary responsibility for spiritual formation belongs to the family. We further compounded the problem by unnecessarily leaving parents out of the loop as we designed and implemented programs for their children. Every year we took their children to camp. When they returned, we provided the parents with little or no information about a week's worth of experiences and curriculum. Even if a parent was interested in building on what we had introduced, they had no idea what we had shared or how to begin. And they weren't made aware of our long-range plans for the spiritual development of their children and students who were attending Lake Pointe.

Changing Directions

I wish I could say that we immediately fixed the problem. We didn't. Our first attempt to substantially change the *status quo* made very little impact. Part of the lack of change had to do with the fact that we assigned the task to an existing middle-management staff member who was overworked, under-resourced, and did not receive a clear strategy for pulling off such a major change. So we tried again, this time we turned the effort into a major, all-church initiative with corresponding attention, calendar, priority, and resources. We also hired the person we believed was most knowledgeable on the issue and who had the capacity and passion to create a reproducible model for local churches everywhere.

In January 2007 my coauthor, Kurt Bruner, joined our staff after a twenty-year ministry with Focus on the Family where he coached local churches on this very subject. He assembled all of the key stakeholders on our staff, each of whom needed to speak into a strategic planning process in order to create a shared vision, buy in, and create workable solutions.

Prior to our first gathering, Kurt invested time discovering the present reality at Lake Pointe Church. We would have felt much better about ourselves if we didn't know some of his findings, but we would have never had the insight needed to put together an effective plan for significant change. Here's what he discovered:

Demographics: We discovered that the vast majority of those stepping onto our campuses each weekend were part of a household that included a married couple with kids living at home. Most leaders from other growing churches report the same demographic reality. This meant that our tendency to avoid overemphasizing family so as not to offend singles was a misfire since couples, parents, and grandparents were our "core customers." Like most churches, we tried to avoid making anyone feel excluded. But a business failing to serve its primary constituency will go out of business quickly.

So, rather than design our ministry language and programs to the exception such as single adults, we learned to accommodate those exceptions while serving the core. The good news is that, despite an unmarried population of nearly 25 percent of the congregation, we have yet to experience any real criticism over our ongoing home ministry emphasis.

Marriages at Risk: We conducted anonymous surveys of our married couples asking them to gauge their relationships based upon two statements . . .

- I believe my marriage will last until one of us dies.
- I believe my marriage is, for the most part, God-honoring and happy.

The second question helped us distinguish between the "grin and bear it" marriages rooted in opposition to divorce and the marriages truly at risk. We discovered that about 20 percent of our most faithful couples were experiencing what we consider "at risk" marriages—pretty important information for a church leadership team to know as it creates strategies for tribal impact.

Parents Confident but Complacent: We asked parents to respond to three statements . . .

- I am confident my child has or will trust Jesus Christ as Savior and Lord by age twelve. (Note: Statistics reveal that the vast majority of lasting faith decisions occur before the teen years.)[1]
- I am confident my teen will remain an active believer in adulthood. (Note: Statistically speaking, about half will not.)[2]

- My family has a routine in which we discuss spiritual beliefs and values.

We discovered that our parents were highly confident their children and teens would have a strong faith, but passive about Christian routines at home. Confidence and complacency are a dangerous combination! We learned that we needed to consistently remind parents and grandparents that no matter how well we did in the 1 to 2 hours we had their kids at church, deep faith roots grow when nurtured in the rich soil of an intentional home.

In addition to specific data about our own families, we make a point of staying informed about the latest trends, studies, news, and cultural influences impacting the world of families. (See Appendix A for a sample overview of key studies and trends.)

As we were launching our initiative, Kurt invited a group of church leaders around the country to innovate in their own settings, so that we could all benefit from one another's discoveries. This alliance of about fifteen churches came together to help create a common vocabulary for what is now in the early stages of becoming a thriving movement. The Strong Families Innovation Alliance included churches from around the nation from various traditions and sizes including megachurch congregations like Willow Creek and Saddleback, Scottsdale Bible, and Lake Pointe. It also included medium to small churches such as Wheaton Bible Church, Ventura Missionary Church, and Sonrise Church in Clovis, California.[3]

The churches involved met together twice a year for two years. During each gathering leaders shared their own present reality, innovative ideas, and discoveries about best practices. They also discussed how to extend lessons learned to other churches, which became the beginning of the growing movement among churches today called Faith@Home.[4] Some of the most important findings of the Alliance are as follows.

1. Family Ministry = Children's Ministry. Unfortunately, when church leaders hear "family ministry," they typically limit their thinking to "children's ministry." As a result, very few develop high-level strategies to drive marriage or parenting intentionality.

2. Marriage Ministry = Annual Event. Similarly, when church leaders hear "marriage ministry," they tend to think of an annual retreat or event rather than an ongoing strategy for building God-honoring marriages.

3. Best Case = Secondary Priority. Most church leaders acknowledge that family-oriented ministry is a second-or third-tier priority in their church.

4. Worse Case = Off Radar Screen. Many churches do not even have a values statement about the home, so programs driving family intentionality are completely off the strategic radar screen.

5. Need = Integrated Strategies. While many churches have created isolated programs for families—often in the form of life-stage classes, which separate rather than integrate family faith experience—what we need are integrated strategies that will create an ongoing culture of intentional families.

So, how do we move toward integrated strategies? We asked the Innovation Alliance to identify ten components that are essential to building a customized strategy for church-driven, family-centered redemption. We consider these the ten essential components to any model.

1. Empower a Visionary Champion: If everyone owns it, no one does. Make it clear which senior leader is responsible for keeping home-driven spiritual formation objectives on the team's radar screen.

2. Establish New Success Measures: What gets measured gets done. Introduce simple measures that will keep you focused on family-centered strategies and drive continual improvement.

3. Build Upon Existing Church Vision: Do not compete with or criticize the existing vision. Build upon it to drive family-centered strategies. Don't call the church to change everything—but to make everything more effective.

4. Build into Existing Church Calendar: Include experiences that will move people toward greater intentionality on the church calendar rather than try to squeeze them in as exceptions or special events. The more "auto-pilot" your family emphasis game plan the easier it will be for everyone.

5. Use "Home" Lens for All vs. Creating New Silo: As a priority, every area of the church must own and apply "faith at home" lenses to every department and program rather than creating another silo competing for attention and resources.

6. Define Success and Call Families to Commitment: Give families a vision of what success at home means and repeatedly call them to commitment and intentionality.

7. Foster a Culture of Family Intentionality: Find ways to communicate the priority and celebrate the practice of families becoming intentional.

8. Customization—One Size Won't Fit All: Every family is unique due to life-season, ages and number of children, marital health, special circumstances, etc. Provide tools that make it easy for families to customize.

9. Invest in Tools for Families: Just like we invest in curriculum for small groups and programs for other ministries, we need to invest in tools that will make it easier for families to do the right thing.

10. Two Degree Strategies: A good plan today is better than a perfect plan tomorrow. It is better to start small and build momentum than try to change everything all at once or achieve complete buy-in from all sectors.[5]

The Lake Pointe Model

Our Lake Pointe team then developed an integrated Faith@Home strategy in light of the lessons we learned during the Innovation Alliance process. We identified two key goals:

1. Make it easy for families to become intentional.
2. Make it more likely they will do so.

Toward that end, we instituted a four-pronged strategy.

Strategy 1: Declaration

We began with a declaration to the congregation. We admitted that we had failed in part to inform them of their discipling responsibilities and that we had unintentionally left them out of the process of the spiritual formation of their own kids. We let the Christian parents of our church know that, in no uncertain terms, it was their responsibility to lead their children to Christ and disciple them. We made it clear that we were not going to do their job for them. We were there to help, but that only they could provide the best opportunity for the spiritual formation of their own children.

Strategy 2: Best-Of Resources

The second part of our effort was to do a better job resourcing our people to build stronger marriages and families by providing the necessary tools for every unique family makeup and season. We live in a time when there are more resources for family and marriage than ever before. What our people really need is someone to be a knowledge broker. They need someone to sort through the mountain of options, recommend the best, and then make them conveniently accessible when they need specific tools for a specific family-season or situation. We identified dozens of unique family types, and then created brochures for each with recommended resources, baby steps for implementation, and existing church ministries and events to help them navigate their current family reality. Here is part of the growing list of "family types or life stage seasons" we have identified and for which we provide helpful guidance:

Single	Preparing for Adolescence	Exploring Adoption
Hope to Marry	Launching Young Adults	Unplanned Pregnancy
Engaged	Empty Nest	Facing Infertility
Building a Strong Marriage	Influencing Grandchildren	Unbelieving Spouse
Considering Children	Raising a Special Needs Child	Family Finances
Preparing for Baby	Single Parents	Addiction
Intentional Parenting	Difficult Teen	Caring for Aging Loved Ones
Leading Your Child to Christ	Blended Families	Grief
Your Child's Schooling Options	Difficult Marriage	Living Together

All of these "life stage" brochures and the recommended resources are housed in a physical space, called *The
HomePointe Center*, in the main foyer of all of our campuses.
In an effort to make it convenient and, therefore, more likely
to be utilized, most of the recommended practical tools
such as date-night ideas, family night activities, mealtime,
bedtime, and movie night chat suggestions are free for the
taking. In addition, other recommended resources including

books, are made available for purchase or can be borrowed at no cost. *The HomePointe Center* serves as a constant reminder to our people that we want to help them keep their family a top priority. Setting aside a valuable piece of church real estate on "Main Street" speaks to the importance of this emphasis in our fellowship. We have also created an online version of *The HomePointe Center* so our people can access all the tools at any time from home, or even on their smartphone. Again, convenience is a vital element of our model.

Strategy 3: Integrated Campaigns

One of the most effective ways we "make it more likely" that families will disciple their children is through the use of all-church campaigns. Several times each year we challenge our people to complete a simple self-assessment and create a simple 120-day plan of intentionality. At the same time, we emphasize one "holy habit" we consider key to spiritual formation in the family.

Our first all-church Faith@Home assessment revealed that prayer was the least likely thing happening in our church members' homes. Everyone considered prayer important. It just was not happening on a regular basis in their homes. In preparation for a campaign on prayer in the home, we discovered several studies that revealed the divorce rate drops dramatically when a couple prays together on a regular basis. Few of our members, however, were actually building prayer into their at-home routines. So our first major campaign was called *Praying Together.* We challenged all of our people to become a "7-5-2" family. We challenged our people to pray *for* their family 7 days a week, pray *with* their family 5 days a week (we let them include mealtime), and if married, pray *with their spouse* after sharing intimate requests at least 2 times per week. We challenged our people to make a 120-day commitment to be a 7-5-2 family. Then, we provided them with free tools that would make starting the routine less intimidating, especially for those who might be new believers or had never prayed in front of anyone.

The prayer campaign was followed by a campaign that emphasized serving together. Then, we emphasized blessing one another at home. Our most recent campaign challenged our people to simply eat more meals together at home. In addition to the two major campaigns each year, we have also launched several mini-campaigns. These mini-campaigns take place in conjunction with recurring seasonal events such as Thanksgiving, Christmas, Mother's Day and Father's Day, Valentine's Day, and summer break, to help families use these occasions to be more intentional about spiritual formation.[6]

Strategy 4: Integrate vs. Disintegrate

The final part of our strategy focused on taking simple steps that would leverage our existing age-graded and family ministries to integrate, rather than disintegrate, the family faith experience. Whenever possible, we try either to include or link the entire family to our age group program offerings. Although it is important to note that we believe it is not what *is* or *is not* happening at the church that is the heart of this movement, but rather what needs to begin to happen in the home.

We asked our staff to rethink all of their existing programming and to inform, educate, and, when possible, invite families to participate at some level. For instance, we make

it possible for parents to watch all of our summer camp services online, while their children are experiencing the same.
The purpose of this effort is to facilitate family discussions
when the students return home. We are also being careful to
add programming at the church only when absolutely necessary and to streamline existing programming to keep from
competing with quality family time.

To date, Lake Pointe has invested close to $500,000 to
design this model and produce the resources where they
did not already exist. Realizing that many churches cannot afford to do what Lake Pointe has done and in order
to be good stewards of what we have learned, we are now
offering this model, the original resources, graphic art, and
campaign materials to other churches. An affordable annual
subscription for the HomePointe model and resources is
made available on a sliding scale so a church of any size can
participate. These subscription fees are then reinvested in
the model to provide continuous improvement to existing
materials, to develop new resources, and new campaigns for
the movement. These resources can also be customized to
reflect a church's particular theology and church "brand."
This is important because each local church is the frontline
of encouragement and support for intentional families.[7] To
date, one hundred churches have adopted the Lake Pointe
Model.

Now three years after the launch of our own Faith@
Home initiative, our leadership has once again evaluated how
well we have been living out our thirteen values. This time
the twelfth value, the value of families playing a key role in
the spiritual formation of their children, moved from dead

last to one of the top three. We are not yet there, but we have begun the journey. We would love for your tribe to join us.

Leading Small Action Plan

Get started applying the concepts explored in this chapter to your church by inviting your leadership team to discuss their answers to the following questions.

Family Tribes

"AS IS" Reality

1. Which category best describes the present reality of your church strategy regarding building strong families?

- **Category One:** We are just beginning to craft a vision for families in order to get these issues on our leadership team's radar screen.
- **Category Two:** We have begun changing existing or creating new programs that will move family from a third-tier to a second-or first-tier emphasis.
- **Category Three:** We have launched a senior leadership team initiative with the goal of developing an integrated strategy for driving faith into the home.

2. List all ministry programs that launch healthy marriages, strengthen existing marriages, or salvage crisis marriages.

3. List all ministry programs that help parents' disciple their own children and/or grandchildren.

4. For each program listed, estimate participation as a percent of typical weekend attendance.

"COULD BE" Dreams

1. Come up with at least twenty ideas of things you could do in the future in order to . . .

- Strengthen existing marriages
- Inspire parents to become intentional at home
- Equip parents to pass the faith
- Partner with parents in passing the faith
- Strengthen parent/teen relationships so kids want parents' faith
- Help families experience God as a unit rather than as isolated individuals
- Leverage family focus to attract unchurched to the church
- Create a culture of family-centered faith at the church

2. How might you create a churchwide culture that infuses Faith@Home priorities into every existing program/process?

3. How could you move all members to become intentional regarding marriage and parenting?

4. How could you cast a compelling vision and create a clear point of entry so it is easy and more likely for families to do the right thing?

"MIGHT BE" Protype

Drawing from these ideas and gleaning from models at other churches, describe a strategy you believe would help this church create a culture of intentional families in the next twelve months.

"SHOULD BE" Priorities

1. In light of your resource and schedule realities, what obstacles do you see to implementation? How might you resolve them?

2. Which elements of the proposed prototype should be top priority for a Phase One initiative?

"WILL BE" Priorities

1. What is the single most important step to be taken during the next 120 days in order to move toward implementation?

2. Who is the lead person responsible for success?

3. What budget/resources will he/she have to accomplish the objectives?

To make it easy to go deeper on the themes of this chapter we have provided a free video overview. Invite your leaders to watch the corresponding segment and come to the next team meeting ready to discuss the "Leading Small Action Plan" questions. Access the video at: TribalChurchBook.com.

Chapter Four

Life Group Tribes

Do you think the apostle Peter was nervous before he preached at Pentecost? How many people do you think he thought would respond to his message? Before you answer, remember, there were no churches, Christian organizations, or church history present when this took place. So what do you think? Twenty-five people? Thirty-five people? A hundred people?

Of course we know that more than three thousand people were saved through that first day of preaching! In other words, the first Christian church was a megachurch from day one. So how did the disciples respond to make sure that everyone was cared for and that the initial explosion of growth did not create a chaotic environment that would hamper the spread of the gospel?

Acts 2:46 tells us one of the keys that allowed the church to go from three thousand to countless millions was tribes: "And every day they devoted themselves to meeting together in the temple, and broke bread from house to house. They ate their food with gladness and simplicity of heart." In other words, from the beginning, the three thousand new converts were divided into small tribes, which met in homes to study together, break bread, and care for each other. This is why it is important for church leaders to understand a second layer of "tribes" at their church, the small group.

At Lake Pointe Church we tell every new member that it is vital for each person to find a small group or "tribe" in which they can become an active participant. This is first communicated at an orientation that is offered once a month on a Sunday evening. The purpose of this three-hour introduction to our fellowship is to help the new member along a clear path of spiritual formation and assimilation. In addition, we share the purpose of the church and expectations of each individual toward fulfilling our mission.

Why make this an emphasis? Because those who only attend the large church gathering tend to remain spectators. By joining a small or even midsize group (which we call Life Groups), they move toward accountability and as a result, greater spiritual maturity. I often say in those settings, "We are not really a large church, we are a collection of small churches, and there is a sense in which you haven't really found your church until you have found a smaller tribe we call Life Groups."

We happen to be a church that believes in on-site, mid-sized tribes as well as small home-based groups. Many other great churches only offer small groups in homes to accomplish the same ends and many of them do so effectively. We have chosen to offer weekly, on-site, midsized Life Groups that meet immediately prior to or following the worship services. These groups further subdivide into off-site Growth Groups that meet once or twice per month in homes. We believe on-site Life Groups are most effective for the following reasons:

1. Time: When someone gives their time to attend a church service on one day and then must give up a second time slot on another day for their small group experience, they are less likely to do so. However, if they can attend their Life Group immediately before or after a service, even if they are on the property for 2½ hours, they consider it only one section of time. The majority of your most-committed people will give you two time slots a week, not three. If two slots are already required by a worship service and a "week night" small group experience, it is hard to get them to commit the third time slot to serve in a ministry. Others may come to service and serve but will not commit the third hour to the vital community they need to experience in the Life Group. As a result, most churches with only off-site small groups average at best 30 to 40 percent of their adult membership. Churches with well-managed on-site, midsized groups can see a participation rate as high as 80 percent.

2. Childcare: Even the best efforts to provide home-based childcare, which range from "find your own childcare" to "stick the kids in a back room" to "one couple misses one out of every five gatherings," fall short. On-site programming for children is easier to make safe, efficient, effective, and convenient. It is also my personal belief that some of our church members who attend Life Groups have not yet really bought into the small group concept, but they attend faithfully just to get a break from their kids for a few hours each week.

3. Fear and Convenience: It is much easier to ask a new church member to walk down the hall and try out a Life Group while they are already in the building than it is to ask them to navigate their way to a home in a strange neighborhood. And here is the reality. If you go into a room to visit a Life Group on-site and you get uncomfortable, if you do not enjoy it, or if it just goes too long, you can always pretend to go to the restroom and not return. This is pretty difficult to pull off in a home unless you are planning to climb out of someone's bathroom window! I have found that many new paradigm churches today only offer small home groups and do not offer midsized on-site groups. The common argument is that they cannot afford the building costs associated with on-site midsized groups. While I understand their concern, I believe that if a larger percentage of their people were assimilated through the use of midsized on-site groups, the necessary resources to provide facilities for such groups would exist. However, in the few parts of the country where land is so expensive that it becomes nearly impossible to provide the necessary facilities for on-site groups, I would suggest a modified on-site midsized group strategy. Here, the church could provide one or two midsized rooms with a capacity of approximately 80 to 100. The church could then invite several small groups that usually meet in homes to join together with other small groups for 4 to 5 weeks, utilizing those rooms before or after existing services and providing on-site childcare. Those who had not yet connected to a small group could then be invited to check out the collection of small groups meeting on the campus for that month. A new collection of small groups could then rotate on campus the following month. The small groups rotating on campus could be from a selected geographical region with various age groups, or they could be a collection of a particular age group from various regions.

4. Group Psychology: It is a very large sociological leap for a person to take who is enjoying the anonymity of a large group of several hundreds or even several thousands to be thrust into a small group of 8 to 10 people. We have found that a midsize group of 25 to 80 allows the person to acclimate more slowly toward greater intimacy and accountability. After people develop trusting relationships, they are more willing to commit to an additional periodic time slot and the more intimate experiences in a home-based small group. By the way, there are some people whose personality profiles make it almost impossible to move them to the smaller setting without first transitioning through the midsize experience.

In short, it takes less time and courage, and there are fewer childcare complexities involved, in attending an on-site midsized group than a small off-site group.

Lake Pointe Life Groups

When Lake Pointe began more than thirty years ago, we started two midsized Life Groups for couples. One group was for those who were over forty years of age and one was for couples younger than forty. In addition, we started one men's Life Group and one ladies' Life Group. This served those who preferred to meet and study the Bible separately from their spouse, those whose spouse refused to attend, or those whose spouse was working in our childcare area at that hour. Today we have a total of 156 midsize, on-site Life Groups that meet each week.

Very quickly we found that more of our people moved into our Life Group tribes when they fully understood the five purposes of these groupings and the needs met there that could not be provided in a larger service format. The first unique purpose of a Life Group is **interactive Bible study**. Obviously a large service format does not allow an abundance of questions and answers, individual application, and then personal encouragement to follow through on biblical insights. Interestingly, this vital interaction is what many people are seeking to avoid by not attending Life Groups.

Some people fear that by attending one of these groups, they will be asked to read aloud, pray aloud, or answer a complex spiritual question about a biblical passage. This is why we guarantee that Life Groups are interactive on the attendees' terms. They can ask any questions they desire and volunteer to give input as they like, but no one will initiate interaction without their prior approval. Life Groups are a safe place to listen and learn on the participants' terms and at their comfort level.

Because interactive Bible study is a part of the Life Group, all of our Life Group teachers are trained to lead Bible study discussions rather than lecture. They are required to serve as an assistant teacher and attend a four-week training course for new leaders before leading a group. Before they can lead their own group, they are also required to fill out a questionnaire that requires them to share their church background, salvation experience, and doctrinal beliefs.

After interning as an assistant, taking the training course, and filling out the questionnaire, they are then interviewed by our board of elders. At that interview they are asked to verbally affirm that they will be faithful in their giving, be loyal to church leadership, and abstain from the appearance of evil. This is in addition to the commitment they are asked to make to support the values of the church and adhere to basic biblical disciplines that should be a part of every fully developing Christian's life.

The process is demanding because, in a lot of ways, as the small group tribe goes, so goes the church. A staff member or lay volunteer then provides continuing coaching to each Life Group leader to foster his or her ongoing development.

Each Life Group has two leaders, the primary teaching leader and the care leader. While the teaching leader is the recognized and primary spokesperson for the group, the care leader is responsible for helping organize members' care and ministry projects as well as facilitating smaller home-based Growth Groups and accountability partnerships.

The second purpose for Life Groups is **fellowship**. God's Word makes it clear how important it is to have close Christian friends. Ecclesiastes 4:9 says "Two are better than one because they have a good reward for their efforts." Life Groups provide the environment in which it is more likely participants will develop lifetime and Christ-honoring relationships. If someone has been a member of Lake Pointe for several years and complains of being unable to develop meaningful friendships, I will ask the person about their

Life Group participation. Life Groups are where those deeper relationships are formed.

One of the disappointments that I have as the pastor of a larger church is that I don't have the opportunity to know everyone in the church. I'm not the only one who feels this tension. One of the complaints I hear from time to time about Lake Pointe is that we are "just such a large church." People are even hesitant to join such a large church for fear that, unlike the church they attended before Lake Pointe, "they won't know everyone."

But large numerical growth doesn't have to exclude meaningful relationships. I love baseball and I love going to see the Texas Rangers play. Over the years the massive size of the crowd has never bothered me. A big crowd usually means the team is on a winning streak (or that it is opening day). Why does it not seem to concern me that I do not "know everyone" at the ballpark? Two reasons: First, I know that I am a part of a larger tribe called Rangers fans and that for the most part—except for those pesky Red Sox and Yankee fans living in our city—most of the people seated around me, even if I do not know their names, are cheering and hoping for the same outcome. Second, I always attend the game with a smaller tribe—my wife, Marsha, and another couple, our grandkids, or three or four buddies who are also Rangers fans.

The baseball metaphor illustrates a similar dynamic that happens in a local church. It does not matter how large the church gets, if you are involved in a smaller tribe or Life Group with which you are experiencing ever-deepening friendships. Building healthy small group tribes is an essential fellowship component to every tribal church.

The third critical activity that occurs in these Life Group tribes is **care.** When someone joins our church family, it is our responsibility to care for that person's spiritual, emotional, and, in some cases, physical needs. But, it is that individual's responsibility to put himself or herself in the place where this kind of care takes place. At Lake Pointe that place is a Life Group. It is the Life Group's care leader whose primary responsibility is to organize the tribe members to care for one another.

I do not know when it happened, but at some time in the history of the church, people began to expect the clergy to do all the ministering. I believe that is why 59 percent of the churches in America have fewer than 100 participants, counting both adults and children.[1] That is about the number of people for whom one person can effectively care. According to Ephesians 4:12, it is the job of those in the pastor/teacher role to equip the saints to minister to one another. Which is also to say, it is not only the responsibility of church members to put themselves in a place to be cared for, but also for them to position themselves to care for others. It is amazing to me that there are those who become concerned when they do not get the attention they feel they need, but then have no concern about the unmet needs of their fellow tribesmen.

Whenever there is a death, sickness, or another kind of crisis in a Lake Pointe member's life, we can tell immediately if that person has a meaningful connection to a Life Group. When I or another staff member show up, if that person is an active Life Group member, we find there is very little—if anything—that needs to be added to the ministry already taking place. The love expressed by the Life Group is both more meaningful and helpful because of the knowledge that comes from everyone involved having done life together deeply. If that person has not connected to a Life Group, we find most times that the ministry from our staff is the entire ministry they receive.

One of the ways we have empowered our leaders and helped them to be seen as true ministers is by encouraging the observance of Communion in Life Groups. In addition, many times Life Group leaders will baptize the members or family members of their own Life Group.

The fourth unique benefit from Life Group involvement is **meaningful service**. All of our Life Groups are commissioned to adopt at least one ministry project for their tribe. Many of our groups have taken on multiple projects, giving their participants a variety of opportunities, including those that are local, national, and international. In other words, Life Group members not only study God's Word together, they also put God's Word into action together. There is a deeper intimacy that comes to a tribe when they serve God together.

When our church first began, the connection between Life Groups and individual ministry involvement was not as strong as it is today. In those early days, if you wanted to serve, you did so in addition to the time spent with your Life Group with those outside of your Life Group. Although some in our congregation still find a place of service outside

of their Life Group, today most of our people serve with
their Life Group.

We have also found that a greater percentage of our
members now serve because of this paradigm shift. They are
now motivated by an opportunity to fellowship with their
tribe, in addition to the feeling of significance that service
brings, and the realization that real needs are met by their
involvement.

Finally, the Life Group is a critical part of the pathway
to **accountability**. As pastor, I feel it is primarily my job to
motivate those who are attending one of our services to
engage with a Life Group. In turn, we expect the leadership
in Life Groups to encourage their members to take the next
step of participating in monthly home-based groups of 8 to
10 people we call Growth Groups. Fellowship, prayer, and
support—rather than Bible study—are the primary activities
of these home gatherings. Some Growth Groups have also
chosen to do ministry projects together for their monthly
gatherings. Over time, it is common for these relationships
to grow into lifelong friendships and same-gender accountability partnerships that help our people grow to be more
like Christ. Proverbs 27:17 says, "Iron sharpens iron, and one
man sharpens another."

Many of our home-based Growth Groups start out much
like a simple supper club. A new Growth Group begins when
the Life Group care leader asks those not already connected
to a Growth Group if they would like to form a group themselves or have their names put in a hat as new Growth Groups
are being formed. It is then perfectly legal, after several
months have passed, for an individual or couple to come back

to the care leader and say, "I have really enjoyed fellowship with the couples (or singles) you put us with; however, we would like to try another Growth Group now so we can meet more people in our Life Group." That, by the way, is code language for "I do not have anything in common with the yahoos you put me with and I would like to be in a different group." As I said, it is perfectly acceptable for individuals or couples to keep changing groups until they find one with which they have a high degree of affinity. Once this takes place, we pray that they can stay with that group until Jesus returns.

At this point you might say, "Steve, are you not afraid that cliques will develop and new people will be left out?" The short answer is no. We will provide new cliques for the new people. There is no forced grouping or forced dividing of groups. Doing life deeply does not happen unless people can choose their own tribe, and this certainly is interrupted when tribes are regularly forced to divide and form new groups.

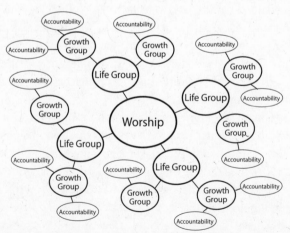

Most of our new Life Groups are formed when several smaller Growth Groups accept the challenge of becoming the core of a new Life Group. The majority of our Life Groups are age-based or life-stage affinity groups, which makes it easier for people to find a fit, (i.e., couples with kids, couples without kids, couples with kids who wish that they didn't have kids, couples in their thirties, couples in their forties, empty-nesters, blended families, families who home-school, single again, and single parents), to name a few. We have also discovered there is even a group in our church whose affinity is "no affinity." They thrive in a mixed group of old and young, single and married, and with and without kids. We provide these "nonaffinity" affinity groups as well.

Recently there has been a flurry of criticism of large churches. A lot of this stems from a reaction to the excesses of numerical idolatry that accompanied some of the disciples of the Church Growth Movement of the late 1980s. But it is important to keep from overreacting to these abuses. While church health is a superior aspiration to church growth, the two are not mutually exclusive. God uses churches of all sizes—big and small—and healthy churches grow. It is God's desire that each church occupies its own unique opportunity and, as the early church did, and that they add "to their number day by day those who are being saved" (Acts 2:47 NASB). Life Groups allow churches to grow larger and have a great impact while still retaining all the positive qualities of a small tribe.

The **interactive Bible study, fellowship, care, meaningful service,** and **accountability** that Life Group tribes provide are part of a truly brilliant plan. However, it is not a plan that

Lake Pointe Church created. In Acts 2, after three thousand were saved on the first day of the first New Testament church, they broke the people into smaller subtribes. They were able to disciple those who had been converted, and God continued to bless them and grew their fellowship.

Leading Small Action Plans

Get started applying the concepts explored in this chapter to your church by inviting your leadership team to discuss their answers to the following questions.

Life Group Tribes

"AS IS" Reality

1. Which category best describes the present reality of your church strategy regarding connecting people to smaller tribes?

- **Category One:** We have never seriously attempted to drive our people into smaller groups.
- **Category Two:** We have implemented one or more models to encourage small group involvement with limited success.
- **Category Three:** A high and growing percentage of our people are involved in a smaller tribe on a regular basis.

2. Summarize your current process for making it easy and more likely people will connect with a smaller tribe.

"COULD BE" Dreams

Come up with at least twenty ideas of things you could do in the future to facilitate a more effective strategy that would . . .

- Create a safe, nonthreatening step toward a smaller group
- Ensure group leaders are qualified and well trained
- Remove the childcare barrier
- Reduce the number of additional time slots required to participate
- Consistently lift high the value of connecting to smaller tribes

"MIGHT BE" Prototype

Drawing from these ideas and gleaning from models at other churches, describe a strategy you believe would help more of your people connect with a small tribe over the coming twelve months.

"SHOULD BE" Priorities

1. In light of your resource and schedule realities, what obstacles do you see to implementation? How might you resolve them?

2. Which elements of the proposed prototype should be top priority for a Phase One initiative?

"WILL BE" Priorities

1. What is the single most important step to be taken during the next 120 days in order to move toward implementation?

2. Who is the lead person responsible for success?

3. What budget/resources will he/she have to accomplish the objectives?

To make it easy to go deeper on the themes of this chapter we have provided a free video overview. Invite your leaders to watch the corresponding segment and come to the next team meeting ready to discuss the "Leading Small Action Plan" questions. Access the video at: TribalChurchBook.com.

Chapter Five

Leadership Tribes

Have you ever found yourself leading a group that, because of its growth and subsequent complexity, made you question your own competence? Have the overwhelming demands of the people to whom you minister ever driven you to the brink of burnout and the temptation to quit? If so, then you can imagine how relieved Moses, who was leading a congregation of three million, must have felt when his father-in-law offered a strategic solution to his leadership limitations.

In Exodus 18, he said, "What you're doing is not good. . . . You will certainly wear out both yourself and these people who are with you, because the task is too heavy for you. You can't do it alone" (vv. 17–18). But Jethro does not stop there. He points Moses' attention to a solution. Jethro states, "But you should select from all the people able men, God-fearing, trustworthy, and hating bribes. Place them over the people, as officials of thousands, hundreds, fifties, and tens" (v. 21).

Moses had failed to identify and utilize one of the most important tribes of any congregation, the leadership tribe. In Ephesians 4:11–12, it explains that the "pastor/teacher" is to "train the saints" to do the ministry. This is not to say that pastors do not do ministry. Rather, it means that as a church becomes larger, the pastor should spend less time doing and more time leading those who are doing. Over time, they should spend a greater percentage of time leading leaders and then finally a greater percentage of time resourcing those who also become leaders of leaders.

When I first became pastor of Lake Pointe, I found myself in a situation like Moses. In those early days, each family in the church was asked to sign up for a designated week to clean the church building. Since the church could not afford to hire a janitor, the members all took turns sweeping the floors and cleaning the bathrooms. Wanting to set a good example, I found myself on one Saturday night—after a full week of seminary classes—cleaning the toilets at the church even though my sermon for the next morning was not finished. The next morning I got up, taught Youth Sunday school for grades 7–12, and then walked over to the auditorium to preach my morning message. Later that summer, I would serve as a counselor for our church at the Association Children's Camp, followed two weeks later by a week at Youth Camp at the same encampment.

If leadership training was the need, I led it. If there was a Tuesday morning prayer time, I arranged and facilitated the gathering. If someone became ill, you could count on Pastor Steve to be at your bedside. I did all the funerals, weddings, baptisms, and led all the Communion services. After all, I was ordained.

The problem with all of this is not simply that I was too busy. The major problem, we discovered, was that my time and energy were bottlenecking our future growth and impact as a church. We did not experience significant growth until I began to step aside and let others do and lead.

Of course, a leader never stops doing ministry. In fact, it is important that a leader never asks his people to do what he is unwilling to do personally. Remaining actively engaged in the work of ministry helps leaders maintain a more realistic expectation of those they lead. But if a church is going to grow, the leader must gradually accomplish more and more through others. In short, leaders must prioritize their own activities and invite those who comprise the leadership tribe in their church to share the load.

Most church staff members desire, for the most part, to earn more pay each year. However, as a general rule, the church should not pay them more for doing the same amount of work. Rather, we should pay more to those who produce more. But there are a limited number of hours in a week, and I do not want our staff to neglect the vital relationships they have with God, family, or friends to do more ministry. That is why in order to achieve more, they must accomplish more through others.

As they shift from doing to leading, and then to leading other leaders, and then finally to resourcing leaders of leaders, they become more valuable to the organization and can accomplish more for the kingdom. Very few churches can afford to hire purely "doers" of ministry. We must hire staff leaders who will accomplish much of their ministry through others.

Early Ministry Season	
60%	Doing ministry
30%	Leading those doing ministry
10%	Leading those who are leading those doing ministry
0%	Resourcing leaders of leaders
100%	Total time
Middle Ministry Season	
30%	Doing ministry
40%	Leading those doing ministry
20%	Leading those who are leading those doing ministry
10%	Resourcing leaders of leaders
100%	Total time
Later Ministry Season	
10%	Doing ministry
30%	Leading those doing ministry
30%	Leading those who are leading those doing ministry
30%	Resourcing leaders of leaders
100%	Total time

Notice in the chart that as time goes by, the leader changes the percentage of time he spends in each category from doing ministry to resourcing others who are leading other leaders. These leaders will in turn hire staff leaders, recruit volunteer leaders, and become responsible for compensating, encouraging, managing, and leading tribes of leaders. The larger the church, the greater the need for more tribes of leaders who can lead their own tribes.

Compensating Your Leaders

Every member of your leadership tribe needs compensation. Not all will be paid with dollars, but all need to be compensated. There are at least ten ways to do this.

The first and most obvious form of compensation is **money**. Because every church has limited resources, it must choose carefully who in the leadership tribe will receive a paycheck. A typical church in America will spend about 50 percent of its general budget on salary and benefits for paid staff.[1]

When consulting other churches, I am often asked "When can we add another paid staff member?" The formula is pretty simple. If your budget is growing by $200,000 a year, you will have 50 percent of that increase or $100,000 of additional money that was not available the prior year to spend on staff. First, you must address any uncontrollable increases like health insurance costs for existing staff. Then you need to address any cost of living or merit raises needed for existing staff. Once you have subtracted those costs from the $100,000, the remaining amount is what you have for salaries and benefits to expand your paid staff.

It is also important to note that it rarely makes sense for everyone on staff to receive the same percentage increase in monetary compensation from year to year. Merit raises should reflect effort, talent, and the value of an employee to the organization. In Marcus Buckingham and Curt Coffman's book, *First, Break all the Rules*, they talk about the importance of not treating all employees the same. They state, "Spend the most time with your top performers. Pay attention to them. Be fair to the right people."[2] In the church context, of course, everyone is to be treated fairly. But it is also true that a greater and greater amount of time, resources, and money should go to those who are doing a better job of helping the church accomplish its purpose.

The second form of compensation available to disburse to the leadership tribe is **public and private praise**. (It is important to note, from this point on, that all the remaining forms of compensation can be used to reward both paid and nonpaid members of your leadership tribe.) Usually a leadership tribe member will prefer either public or private praise.

If you publicly recognize an employee or volunteer whose preference is private praise, you really have not paid that person. In fact, the person may consider it a painful experience. In the same vein, if you write a very detailed note of affirmation to one who would prefer to be recognized in front of his or her peers, that person will not feel adequately compensated.

One staff member who has worked for Lake Pointe for many years has kept every note of affirmation that I have written to him. Yet, he finds it very painful to be publicly recognized. He has specifically asked that I not subject him to that "embarrassment." Another staff member asked when I was going to recognize her in our staff meeting for a major milestone—ten-year anniversary—so that she could invite her family members to the presentation. Leaders have to find these things out about their leaders and act accordingly if they want to effectively compensate them.

The third form of compensation for leaders is **access**. There are people who are primarily motivated to serve by personal access to the senior leader. In other words, they are willing to contribute to the cause and consider the main perk being able to "hang out" with the leader. This relational aspect seems to be especially important to the Baby Busters and succeeding generations.

I have always exercised an open-door policy for staff. If I am not preparing a message, conducting a strategic planning meeting, or counseling, staff members may walk into my office without an appointment. However, over the years as the church has become larger and my daily schedule has become more crowded, I have found the need to be proactive in scheduling times when I am accessible.

It is very important to have regularly scheduled meetings with your direct reports. One of the reasons many staff meetings go too long is that not enough one-on-one meetings have been held. Every Monday we have a staff meeting, which is attended by our entire staff. This weekly meeting usually lasts about twenty-five minutes. The reason it is so short is that there are very few things about which our entire staff needs to meet. The large staff meeting is followed by a handful of called "sidebars" to discuss the topics about which only the invited participants are concerned. Monthly one-on-one meetings with direct reports also allow me to cover issues without wasting the time of the rest of the staff.

Every month I schedule a special lunch with new staff members. This gives me the chance to put names to new faces, as well as begin to imprint new staff with the Lake Pointe DNA. I also meet for lunch monthly with a group of 6 to 8 existing staff members, which are selected randomly from different levels and departments. This meeting provides an opportunity to answer their questions, find out about their personal lives, and become more aware of what is taking place in their ministries. The lunch also allows the staff members the opportunity to get to know people from other departments and appreciate the work they are doing.

Once a quarter I also have a lunch with our "young guns," who are leadership and staff specialists under the age of forty. During that time together I do as much listening as I do talking. It is very encouraging to hear them share what is going on in their ministry areas. Sometimes I will share my latest leadership lessons or give a mini book review. I also remind them that my e-mail and text box are open and that I want to hear from them. I encourage them to ask questions that I commit to answer within twenty-four hours, make suggestions that I reserve the right to ignore, and "FYI" me on stuff they think I should know.

Lunches and breakfasts are also regularly scheduled with key contributors and key church leaders. At these meals I like to ask these questions:

- Is there any way that Lake Pointe can do a better job of ministering to you and your family?
- Do you have any questions or suggestions about the direction of our church? (One of the key complaints of key contributors is that they are always being asked for money but are rarely asked for input about how the money is spent.)
- How can I pray for you and/or your family?

Gordon MacDonald warns that "an overage of exposure" to any one kind of person sets up an imbalance in your life. In his book *Renewing Your Spiritual Passion*,[3] he lists five different categories of people:

1. *VRPs (Very Resourceful People)*. They ignite our passions. These are mentors.
2. *VIPs (Very Important People)*. They share our passions. These are team members.
3. *VTPs (Very Trainable People)*. They catch our passions. These are the people we are mentoring.

4. *VNPs (Very Nice People)*. They enjoy our passions. These people are merely spectators.
5. *VDPs (Very Draining People)*. They sap our passions. While it is sometimes necessary to deal with these people, we must be careful to limit their access so they do not dominate our time and deplete us.

Very draining people have a tendency to draw you into their vortex of complaints. When VDPs complain, I am tempted to spend an inordinate amount of time explaining our rationale or seeking to convince them that the church's strategy is on the right course. I have learned over the years to just resort to what I now call the "matador." When a bull charges a matador, the matador does not stand in the bull's path and risk getting gored. He simply steps to one side and lets the wild beast run through his cape. When high-maintenance people complain, and I know they will never be won over, I simply reply: "Thank you so much for your candid feedback. We will take it into our future considerations." Limiting the time I spend trying to convince the "inconvincible" leaves time to invest in leaders who can make a difference in the lives of others.

While access to leaders will look different in each size church and in each church culture, the key is to be proactive in reaching out and spending time with your leadership tribe.

The fourth tool in your compensation toolkit is similar to the third. Leaders want to add value through **input**, which is the right to contribute ideas before major decisions are made. Those with this preference do not have to have their way, but they do appreciate having their way considered.

When this form of compensation is given, it creates a "win-win." As a rule, leaders make better decisions than committees, but they need accurate data with which to make those decisions. When leaders seek counsel from implementers of those decisions, they make more informed decisions.

Some of the best information, suggestions, and insights have come from the administrative assistants who serve on our staff. These are the people who are answering the phones and talking to our people every day. They hear the squeaks and know where the oil needs to be applied long before anyone else on our staff. There are some in the leadership tribe who will stay engaged because they helped create the vision and therefore have greater buy-in.

The fifth form of compensation is **added responsibility**. One of the long-serving staff members on my team finds great encouragement when we expand his scope of responsibility. He sees that expansion as an expression of trust and an affirmation of his evolving skills and experience. It is important to note here, however, that we must be careful to avoid giving one supervisor too many direct reports. More responsibility does not necessarily mean more people to supervise. More responsibility could be a higher level of influence or oversight and actually involve fewer direct reports, especially as the leader is evolving into a leader of leaders.

Some of our higher-level leaders have fewer direct reports today than they did a decade ago. As a result, their management load has been freed up so they can resource other leaders outside of our church. One example would be my coauthor, Kurt Bruner, Pastor of Spiritual Formation.

Because we believe the Faith@Home movement is so critical, we actually decreased his direct reports this year so that he could give more attention to writing, speaking, and consulting in order to share the HomePointe model with churches around the world.

The sixth currency is that of **significance**. Some consider it important for their leader to periodically remind them of the eternal significance of their work. This is true among staff leaders, but especially true with volunteers.

One of the more difficult ministries to keep staffed at most churches is the preschool and children's ministry. At Lake Pointe, we average three births a week. This means that—come rain or shine—we create a new nursery class every thirty days. There is a command in the book of Genesis to "be fruitful, multiply, fill the earth" (Gen. 1:28). Our people have that one down!

From time to time in a public service, I tell a true story of a man or woman who, after attending our church recently, became a believer. I then explain the main reason that person returned time and time again was because of our children's ministry. The individual at first did not think he or she had a need for church but came back because of their kids' positive experiences and continued to be drawn back. As a result, that individual heard the gospel and made a commitment to follow Christ.

As pastor, I get a lot of undeserved credit for life transformation. I explain that many times the unsung heroes of life-changing and family-changing stories are those who work with our kids each week.

You see, when volunteers work with two-year-olds, they may or may not be aware of the vital role they play in reaching individuals and families for Christ. It is easy to forget the significance of the role they play after several months of being spit up on and after crawling around on the floor picking up soggy pieces of Ritz crackers. They need a leader to remind them that what they are doing makes a big difference for eternity. Rocking a baby while singing "Jesus loves me," or helping a second grader find the book of Matthew, could make the difference between eternal life and death for someone. Significance is a powerful paycheck!

The seventh form of compensation is **empowerment**. When we give leaders authority to make critical decisions concerning their areas of responsibility, within reasonable and clear parameters, we communicate trust and confidence in their abilities. This is known as the responsibility/authority balance; the more responsibility you give to people, the more corresponding authority they should receive.

Many years ago a man in our church gave what, at the time, was a substantial gift to the church. He requested that it not be put in the general fund. Instead, he wanted me to disburse it to those who needed money for resources that had not been budgeted or for unexpected needs or opportunities.

Over the next few years, I became a kind of "Santa Claus Supervisor," who was able to grant legitimate requests for one-time ministry resource needs. As our church grew, it occurred to me, that it would communicate a great deal of confidence "compensation" if I doled out multiple pools of those funds to some of our leaders of leaders, allowing *them* to decide the best ways to invest those funds within their own leadership tribes.

Sometimes empowerment comes in the form of a revised job description that frees employees or volunteers from tasks outside of their gifting and/or passion, so they may expend their energy in a more laser-like fashion. Many times traditional groupings of job responsibilities get us in trouble.

In the church where I grew up, the minister of music was also in charge of all the communication pieces such as the weekly bulletins, church newsletter, church advertisements, and other print jobs. But what if the worship leader has no interest in those areas or, even worse, is incompetent to manage them? To be sure, all of us have parts of our jobs with which we would rather not deal. That is part of what it means to live in a "weed-infested world." However, when possible, it makes good sense and is effective stewardship to keep job descriptions fluid, so that consideration may be given to workloads, passions, and unique abilities of each staff member.

Of course, effective delegation means more than handing a job to someone else in order to get it off your to-do list. I have witnessed supervisors attempting to empower others only to find that certain tasks are not accomplished with excellence. This may not be because the employee who was given the assignment is incompetent, but rather is a failure in the process of delegation. I recommend three critical steps in the delegation process.

First is the need for **clear communication of vision and values**. Most often this is where the handoff is dropped. The necessary time is not invested on the front end to ensure that the leader who is being empowered knows the exact goal of the task, nor does he know the values to which he must adhere in fulfilling that vision. But, even when a clear vision and values are communicated, the second key, **absolute truthtelling**, is necessary. No matter how well vision, goals, and parameters are communicated, there will always be a need to redirect and clarify.

When that need arises, we must inform the empowered leader of the need for a course correction. Many times in a church—and especially with volunteers—we tend to withhold critical information and express our displeasure about an individual's performance to everyone but to the one person who needs to hear it. This misdirection of communication is not only ineffective in empowering the leader, but it is a violation of Scripture, which commands in Ephesians 4:15 that we are to "speak the truth with love."

The final key to empowering delegation is **contact without control**. Some simple form of feedback is needed to allow the supervisor to know the progress of the project and to confirm its alignment with the stated vision and values. The vehicle of communication should be established so that the supervisor has enough information to track progress. But this should not be done in a manner that is cumbersome to the person who is entrusted with the task or that tempts the supervisor to micromanage. Many effective leaders use what we call the 15/5 approach. A project owner is asked to provide a weekly or monthly update that can be written in fifteen minutes and communicated in five minutes. Early stages of a project may require weekly updates, which eventually turn into monthly meetings as things move forward and momentum is established.

I ask all of my direct reports to provide a similar accounting when I meet with them for their monthly one-on-one meeting. I ask them to provide on one sheet of paper the answers to three questions:

1. What have you been working on the past thirty days and what progress has been made?
2. What key projects will you give attention to in the next thirty days?
3. What can I do as your supervisor to help you be successful?

The report does not need to be formal and can be comprised in a simple format of bullet points and/or lists. A good delegation process frees the employee to be fully empowered.

---

3 Keys to Delegation

1. Clear vision and values
2. Truth telling
3. Contact without control

An eighth motivator is **adequate resources** in the form of equipment, budget, facilities, or staff. Many years ago I asked our worship leader, Danny Davis, to tell me his primary motivation for doing ministry at Lake Pointe rather than elsewhere. At that time my list of forms of compensation consisted of seven items. I asked him to pick from those seven and he said his was not on the list, to which I responded that the seven compensations comprised the list and he had to pick one (I was kidding). He explained that his primary motivation was when the church provided him the right equipment and adequate staff with which to do his job with a standard of excellence that he felt honored God. For Danny, and for many other leaders, true compensation means having the resources to do the job well.

The ninth form of compensation is what I call **perks and bonuses**. These are the value-added benefits that come from being in the tribe that you, as a generous leader, oversee. These can take many forms. Birthdays and staff anniversaries provide a great opportunity to give nontaxable gifts to employees and volunteers. At this time the IRS will allow a gift up to $100 without taxes. We give out gift cards for car washes, meals, and retail establishments, such as Target or Home Depot.

As high-visibility leaders, occasionally perks such as sports tickets or vacation homes are made available to us. When we pass these on to our team members, it shows that we understand it is not just one person that accomplishes the work, it is a tribe.

When the financial condition of the church allows, I believe it is important to reward key staff members with a one-time bonus in addition to regular cost-of-living and merit raises. A one-time bonus can be used to acknowledge extra effort given for a nonrecurring project or a season of extra work without adding to the ongoing compensation of an employee. It also adds a dimension of understanding that extra pay must be earned by extra effort each year.

The tenth and perhaps the most valuable form of compensation is **knowledge**. When we invest in the growth of a leader's knowledge, we expand that person's skills and affirm his potential. One effective approach is to recommend or give books that you have read and consider beneficial based on your knowledge of the individual and his or her responsibilities. When you give an outstanding book, it provides value on several levels. One value is the cost of the book itself. Another is the fact that you have read several books (some not so great) and have identified one worth taking the time to read. The win for both the church and the individual is that this new knowledge helps the leader become more effective as a volunteer or paid staff. I never go to a lunch or breakfast with key volunteers without taking a book to give them. We have a large closet in my office where I keep at least a dozen copies of the best books I have read. My assistant keeps a record of which books I have given to each key volunteer.

Knowledge can also be imparted by providing church leadership with a budget for training and seminars, including outside conferences and on-site training. In addition, supervisors should always impart the wisdom they have gained from their own experiences, reading, and conferences, and pass it on to their teams.

We believe that leaders and volunteers need both formal curriculum-based training and in-service personal mentoring. In our leadership school, we offer four general courses for all leaders. Each course is around three hours in length.

1. Lake Pointe Vision and Values
2. Biblical Leadership
3. Leading a Team
4. Becoming a Leader of Leaders

These courses have all been offered for years in a Saturday morning format; however, we are now in the process of recording all of them so they may be offered online and thereby accessed more conveniently.

When I first began ministry as a youth minister in Abilene, Texas, my pastor, Dr. James Flamming, was extremely good at sharing knowledge. Many times he called me into his office to brief me on a leadership issue the church had just experienced. On one occasion he called me in to ask if I knew how to hire a church staff member. He had just completed the process, and he walked me through it while it was still fresh on his mind. The information he shared that day proved invaluable later in my ministry when I pastored my own church. Knowledge sharing is a mark of all effective tribal leaders.

Pay Your Leaders

1. Money
2. Public or private praise
3. Access
4. Input
5. Increased responsibility
6. Significance
7. Empowerment

8. Adequate resources
9. Perks and bonuses
10. Knowledge

How do you know the preferred form of compensation your paid staff and volunteers desire? You ask them. When asked and provided with options, they will tell you their leadership love language. The list I have shared with you is certainly not exhaustive. It has been expanded over time, and I am certain it will be revised in the future.

Over my study desk I keep a list of my direct reports and their top three self-reported compensation preferences. Additionally, I have asked them to solicit the same information from their own leadership tribes and then use that information to pay their leaders and volunteers.

What would you do if you went to work every week and never received a pay check? In time, you would feel unappreciated and undercompensated. You would eventually quit. It is no wonder that some of our volunteer leaders do the same. They have never been paid by the leader of their tribe.

Leading Small Action Plans

Get started applying the concepts explored in this chapter to your church by inviting your leadership team to discuss their answers to the following questions.

Leadership Tribes

"AS IS" Reality

1. Which season best describes the present leadership reality of your ministry?

Early Ministry Season	
60%	Doing ministry
30%	Leading those doing ministry
10%	Leading those who are leading those doing ministry
0%	Resourcing leaders of leaders
100%	Total time
Middle Ministry Season	
30%	Doing ministry
40%	Leading those doing ministry
20%	Leading those who are leading those doing ministry
10%	Resourcing leaders of leaders
100%	Total time

Later Ministry Season	
10%	Doing ministry
30%	Leading those doing ministry
30%	Leading those who are leading those doing ministry
30%	Resourcing leaders of leaders
100%	Total time

2. Summarize your current strategy for leadership recruitment, training, and affirmation.

3. Describe your present approach to rewarding staff and volunteer leaders.

"COULD BE" Dreams

1. Come up with at least twenty ideas of things you could do in the future in order to facilitate a more effective strategy that would . . .

- Identify leadership roles appropriate for nonpaid staff
- Discover nonsalary "pay" preferences of staff and volunteers
- Better motivate, resource, and affirm existing volunteers
- Give more nonsalary "pay" to staff and volunteers

"MIGHT BE" Prototype

Drawing from these ideas and gleaning from models at other churches, describe a strategy you believe would help your leaders work smarter rather than harder.

"SHOULD BE" Priorities

1. In light of your resource and schedule realities, what obstacles do you see to implementation? How might you resolve them?

2. Which elements of the proposed prototype should be top priority for a Phase One initiative?

"WILL BE" Priorities

1. What is the single most important step to be taken during the next 120 days in order to move toward implementation?

2. Who is the lead person responsible for success?

3. What budget/resources will he/she have to accomplish the objectives?

To make it easy to go deeper on the themes of this chapter we have provided a free video overview. Invite your leaders to watch the corresponding segment and come to the next team meeting ready to discuss the "Leading Small Action Plan" questions. Access the video at: TribalChurchBook.com.

Chapter Six

Elder Tribe

There are a lot of details that we do not know about the early church. We don't know how they handled staff meetings, how they handled prospects, or their order of service, just to name a few. But there are other aspects of church life, like leadership, that are extremely clear in the Scriptures.

One of the most critical leadership tasks that the early church accomplished was the appointment of elders, a small, but significant tribe. Every time a church was planted, elders were immediately commissioned with a special leadership task. Acts 14:23 states the apostles appointed "elders in every church."

The first five years of its existence, Lake Pointe was not elder led. Instead, we were a staff-led church. One day I became convicted that our lack of balanced accountability was neither wise nor biblical. So I approached our congregation and asked them to affirm the names of six nonstaff leaders, who would serve as our first board (what we call our elder tribe). Part of my criteria for choosing the individuals was they were people who loved their pastor and loved the Lord even more.

Over the last twenty-six years, our board has been a great source of input, encouragement, and accountability. None of the board members are on staff, besides me. We do have senior staff who attend every board meeting and are free to contribute, but they are not voting members of the board. As lead pastor, I serve on the board by virtue of my office. Each year at least one elder rotates off the board after serving a maximum of five years, enabling us to have fresh voices without sacrificing continuity. Our current bylaws allow up to nine elders, although we currently only have seven, including the lead pastor. The existing elder board nominates new board candidates, which are then confirmed by a secret ballot by our congregation at our annual business meeting.

The process of selecting a name to be presented to the congregation is an important one. Early each August the existing elder board solicits nominations from all of our church leaders. The list is first narrowed by checking the giving record of those submitted. The remaining names are reviewed by the board. Then a secret ballot takes place in which each board member is given the option of writing down the name(s) of any person(s) they would like to eliminate from the final list. This allows any elder to block any person they know they could not in clear conscience recommend to the congregation, without having to criticize them to the other elders or divulge any confidential knowledge about the person. They may choose to eliminate them for any legitimate reason, including but not limited to their tenure in our church, lack of gifting to serve on the board, or their character. This means, as a voting member of the elders, I cannot control who serves on the board, but I can control who does not serve on it.

The remaining list of candidates is discussed and then voted on by the board. While there are no hard and fast rules, we do seek to have a variety of ages on the board, and we try to have at least one attorney, a businessperson, and when possible, at least one elder besides myself with theological training. Although it would be impossible to have a representative from every campus, we do try to have at least one elder from one of our community campuses. This helps us think about our church from that perspective.

Although the board retains veto authority over any staff decision, their primary roles are that of setting policy, exercising church discipline, and direct supervision of the lead pastor. None of the board oversees directly any ministry area, since this would mean that a staff member would have more than one supervisor. As lead pastor, I serve as the liaison between the board and the staff. Each year the board gives a written evaluation of the lead pastor and determines his salary. The lead pastor then has primary responsibility to lead the staff. We describe Lake Pointe's polity as: congregational-ruled, elder-led, and staff-managed.

I know several church leaders who do not have a board, or the boards they have are made up of staff members who are subject to the pastor's authority. I believe this happens many times because of their past bad board experience, fear of loss of freedom, or because the pastor does not want any accountability. When we were developing our board policies, we relied heavily on *Boards That Make a Difference* by John Carver.[1] A couple of the best recent books on the topic of boards are *The Imperfect Board Member* by Jim Brown[2] and *Sticky Teams* by Larry Osborne.[3]

One of the key dangers for boards is the temptation to micromanage, which does not allow staff leaders to do their jobs or execute the responsibilities for which they were hired. Micromanaging boards come about partially due to the fact that elders have not been properly trained in regards to their roles. When an elder joins our board, he is given a detailed policy about the board and its relationship to the pastor. This policy, included in the appendix, was developed several years ago to clarify the role of the elders related to the pastor. I have found this extremely helpful in providing a job description for the elders so they do not come onto the board with an expectation that they are going to manage the church or that any individual elder has authority over the pastor. The elder policy sets out the fact that the board speaks as a unified voice and not as individual voices. Board members are also asked to read several books on boards, so that they are working out of the same mind-set and culture as the existing board.

The board is required by our constitution to meet at least once a month, but it usually meets twice a month. The meetings last about two hours. One meeting a month, we start thirty minutes early to give a greater amount of time to prayer. A typical meeting consists of prayer, reviewing statistics from the past two weekends, reviewing any staff changes, interviewing potential Life Group leaders, interviewing candidates for ordination, interviewing candidates for ministry leadership, discussing church discipline situations, setting church policy when needed, and giving input on miscella-neous issues brought by the pastor or other senior staff. In each meeting, time is also spent on elder enrichment of some kind, such as a book review or other type of study. From time to time, church members come to an elder meeting to be anointed with oil, and the elders pray for them to be healed. Once a month the elders select an all-church prayer focus and review the pastor's reading list. Once a year the elders evaluate the lead pastor and set his salary and give input on the other staff salaries before they are finalized. The elders also give input concerning the annual budget prepared by staff before it is passed to the congregation for approval at the annual business meeting. Every February the board reviews and makes any necessary adjustments to the church's current policies and procedures for its pastor succession plan.

The board rarely votes on anything. On most issues we discuss an issue and then arrive at a consensus. I respect the elder tribe so much that if there is any major pushback from them on an initiative that I have proposed, I slow down, back up, or rework the proposal. In the same way, the elders respect my opinion and unique vantage point such that if I have concerns about anything they propose, they also will reconsider their position.

Select board members have various areas of responsibil-ity including elder development, prayer, elder fellowship, community campus liaison, and liaison to the pastor. Having a pastor liaison allows me to communicate private concerns about my role as an employee to one board member. We have found that an individual representing the board provides a better accountability partner than does a group. To further clarify the role of the pastor liaison, the following guidelines were recently adopted:

Lead Pastor Spiritual Protection Policy

1. The Lead Pastor, like all Christians, is called to be holy, maintaining spiritual and moral purity.
2. Moral failure by the Lead Pastor would be detrimental to the spiritual well-being of the Lead Pastor and his family and could have significant and far-reaching negative consequences on the cause of Christ and Lake Pointe Church.
3. God's power, through the saving love of His Son, Jesus, is the only and sufficient hope of spiritual and moral purity. The Lead Pastor, the Elder serving as Pastor Liaison, and the Elder Board will actively seek God's protection of the Lead Pastor. The tools with which God has equipped His people (Bible, prayer, accountability, confession, safeguards, etc.) will be actively engaged in the battle to protect the Lead Pastor.
4. The Lead Pastor is primarily responsible for his spiritual and moral purity and should develop and consistently maintain safeguards to protect against temptation and moral failure.
5. The Elder serving as Pastor Liaison is responsible for encouraging the Lead Pastor in pursuit of spiritual and moral purity, monitoring the effectiveness of the Lead Pastor's system of spiritual and moral safeguards, and where necessary in the best interest of the Lead Pastor,

his family or the Church, confront the Lead Pastor about such issues.

6. In performing his duties, the Pastor Liaison should encourage the Lead Pastor in establishing appropriate safeguards and monitor the effectiveness of the Lead Pastor's moral safeguards by:

- Regularly communicating with the Lead Pastor;
- Regularly praying for the Lead Pastor and encouraging others to also;
- Staying informed about the Lead Pastor's habits, travel, calendar, work load, exercise of spiritual disciplines, family time, Sabbath, quiet time, and similar issues;
- Verifying that the Lead Pastor is maintaining a current and effective accountability relationship with at least one other male;
- Systematically communicating discreetly, respectfully, and confidentially according to an acceptable protocol with persons of significance in the life of the Lead Pastor, possibly including his administrative assistant, senior staff, spouse, accountability partner(s), and travel companions;
- Taking such other reasonable, biblically-based actions as may be appropriate to support, encourage, and protect the Lead Pastor.

7. Information concerning the Lead Pastor disclosed in confidence by the Lead Pastor to the Elder Liaison should be kept confidential except in dire circumstances.

Creating a tribe of elders was one of the best moves Lake Pointe has ever made. I do not know where we would be today without our board's input and leadership. With our elders' support, I can—as pastor—lead with greater boldness. Also, it allows me to learn when an idea is bad in front of a half-dozen individuals rather than several thousand. Another thing to keep in mind is if the lead pastor is hit by a milk truck, the congregation is protected from a less-than-benevolent dictator who may be the next pastor, and the vision and doctrine of the church is protected by more than just one person.

Of course, elder tribes can be dysfunctional. Dysfunctional elder boards operate in one of two problematic ways: they either rubber-stamp decisions or they bottleneck ministry. Yet, when board members have been carefully and prayerfully selected and trained, and trust and mutual respect are nurtured and protected, the church and its mission are well served. A healthy elder tribe—more than any other leadership tribe—is the key to the church's long-term impact.

Leading Small Action Plan

Get started applying the concepts explored in this chapter with your church by inviting your leadership team to discuss their answers to the following questions.

The Elder Tribe

"AS IS" Reality

1. Which category best describes the present reality of your church with regard to the governing elder body?

- **Category One:** We have no governing board or rely purely on congregational votes for important decisions.
- **Category Two:** We have a governing body, but it does not function in a productive or healthy manner.
- **Category Three:** We have a strong board with a good understanding of their role.

2. Summarize your current approach to making sure the pastor has enough authority balanced by healthy accountability.

"COULD BE" Dreams

Come up with at least twenty ideas of how a healthy board should serve the congregation and protect the pastor.

"MIGHT BE" Prototype

Drawing from these ideas and gleaning from models at other churches, describe any changes you would recommend to the current process of governance at your church.

"SHOULD BE" Priorities

1. In light of your cultural and political realities, what obstacles do you see to implementing any of the changes? How might you resolve them?

2. Which elements should be top priority for a Phase One effort?

"WILL BE" Priorities

1. What is the single most important step to be taken during the next 120 days in order to move toward a stronger governance situation?

2. Who is the lead person responsible for success?

3. What budget/resource/political challenges will he/she face?

To make it easy to go deeper on the themes of this chapter we have provided a free video overview. Invite your leaders to watch the corresponding segment and come to the next team meeting ready to discuss the "Leading Small Action Plan" questions. Access the video at: TribalChurchBook.com.

Chapter Seven

Generation Tribes

Lake Pointe Church was launched in the summer of 1979, primarily by those who came from the Builder Generation (those born from 1925–1945). They had a strong desire to reach the up-and-coming Baby Boomer tribe (those born 1946–1964). But early on in their ministry, they recognized that every generation was its own tribe. Boomers at that time dominated the population of starter homes surrounding the area where Lake Pointe was planted. The original core group of our church believed that when they hired me, a twenty-six-year-old seminary student, as their first pastor, that I would no doubt attract others from my own generation.

Early on we decided Lake Pointe would lean forward to the next burgeoning Boomer Generation rather than back to the older Builders. There were plenty of churches in our area with a more traditional and formal style that appealed to the Builder Generation. Even though Lake Pointe, like many other new churches at the time, was heavily influenced by both the Willow Creek "seeker-driven" model[1] and the Saddleback "purpose-driven" model,[2] we were neither. But we did glean from the genius of both of those two churches in contextualizing to the culture in which we lived. That is why we developed our own unique, biblical paradigm to be a culturally relevant church.

At a conference that I attended in Plano, Texas, back in the 1980s, I heard George Barna say that church growth is not so much a set formula as it is "a series of sensitive and creative responses to a changing environment." I believe that the changing environment to which we must respond is made up of three components:

1. Our understanding of the mind of God
2. The makeup of the local church body
3. The community the church is seeking to reach

The last two are heavily influenced by generational issues.

Lake Pointe quickly evolved from a church of Builders seeking to reach Boomers to a church of Boomers led by a Boomer leader seeking to reach Boomers. Operating as a one-generation-focused church in those early days simplified many things and made a lot of our choices rather obvious.

Another dynamic that influenced Lake Pointe in the early days was my religious résumé and specific gifts. Although I had grown up a Southern Baptist, I had worked as a regional director for Young Life during my college days in West Texas. As a result of working in a parachurch organization, I was exposed to a variety of people from a cross section of Christian traditions and generations. I came to appreciate the strengths and observe the weaknesses of various approaches to ministry, helping me better understand that there might be more than one way to do church. Working with unchurched young people forced me to become a student of their culture and contextualize the gospel.

My spiritual gifts are leadership, teaching, and evangelism. Evangelism became my motivation, while leadership and teaching became the tools to change what did not make sense or what might limit the church's impact.

A Little Thing That Made a Big Difference

About five years into our journey, it occurred to me that there were more and more people we were trying to reach who either could not afford or did not like to wear the clothes that I grew up calling "our Sunday best." I remember the first Sunday on which I decided not to wear a suit and tie to a weekend service. Several members approached me prior to the service and asked me if I was speaking that day. Although they made no reference to my attire, I knew it gave rise to their question. I told them I was indeed teaching, but also made no comment about my clothing.

I was very surprised at the number of positive comments I received during the following week, like, "Pastor Steve, that was so cool. I'm sure my neighbors would come to church if they didn't have to dress up." The following week I wore my regular coat and tie, having decided that I would go casual about once every six weeks to help a segment of those we were trying to reach feel more comfortable. I was once again surprised, this time by the disappointment of our people that a permanent change of the dress code had not taken place. In addition to those who had limited resources for clothes, it appeared there were those who were required to dress more formally for work and were hoping for a more casual standard at their church. One man even told his wife that he was likely to attend church more often if he did not have to dress up like he was forced to do at his job. Unlike the generation of Builders who preceded us, dressing up to go to church was not viewed as much as respect for God as it was for being inauthentic. Many in the succeeding generations that we are currently reaching would now consider formal attire as downright heretical.

In many nondoctrinal issues, like attire, we have learned that you have to lean to one generational tribe or another. The same is true for music. Although we had our own version of the worship wars over style and volume of music, it was nothing compared to what some churches experience. We discovered that music style is not a purely generational issue. There are some Boomers who grew up in traditional churches and still find the old hymns to be their most meaningful expression of choral worship. To some extent, that is why in the early years, we began with what has been described by some as a "blended" style of worship. It evolved over the years to a more contemporary, or what I would call "authentic" style. I define "authentic" style as the one that best reflects the natural, everyday music style of most of the church's participants. In some communities the natural music style will be more contemporary, and in other places more traditional. For some, it is heavy on the instrumental; for others, it is more unplugged. In some settings, it is guitar-driven, while in others it is keyboard-driven. The options and combinations of components are almost endless.

If you are a leader of a church, you already know there is nothing as emotional or contentious as people's preferences of styles of worship music. I truly believe that in some churches it would be easier to drop the third person of the Trinity than to change the music style. Over the years we did lose people who either did not like our music style or casual dress. One lady who visited our church in those early years asked one of our greeters, "Doesn't your pastor have any better clothes to wear?" The greeter responded kindly but ended up drawing for her a map to another church in the area, complete with a list of their service times. One of the tough lessons a leader of any church must learn is that you cannot make everyone happy and sometimes you must choose who you lose.

Now I do not mean to suggest that you choose to ignore an entire generation that may already be in your church. It is hardly fair to come into an existing multi-generation church and abruptly cater to just one generation. However, I do believe all churches choose who they lose. A church can choose to let the most prominent generation dictate everything and lose the next generation, or they can lead the existing dominant generation in the spirit of Christ to share their church with and serve the next generation.

Of course, there are several options available to navigate these sometimes perilous generational waters. Some churches have approached the music style challenge by providing choices, offering multiple styles of worship music at different hours. Other churches have sought to combine a variety of styles in the same service. My opinion is that there is actually a very small niche that enjoys or will tolerate such an eclectic approach. Many times, in an effort to please everyone, you instead make everyone unhappy.

Targeting Generations

Should you target one generation within your greater church? Some leaders have decided to do this. Willow Creek Church, for instance, was one of the notable pioneers of this strategy with their AXIS[3] ministry. AXIS not only had its own service, but in many other ways it operated as a semiautonomous church. I say semiautonomous because the ministry still reported directly to Willow's elders and senior leadership team and was responsible to pursue the same overall mission, vision, and values of the church. They were, however, given great leeway to strategically develop their own small group matrix and unique programming while still holding to Willow's purpose of *turning irreligious people into fully devoted followers of Christ*. Willow later abandoned this separate generations approach.

McLean Bible Church in Virginia created Frontline[4] in 1994, to reach the twenties and thirties age group. This church within the church currently averages about twenty-five hundred each week on several campuses across the region. The mother church, which runs about ten thousand, also meets at a variety of satellite campuses. What is interesting is that at some of the satellite campuses there exists both a main McLean traditional church and a younger Frontline service, and at other campuses there is only a main traditional church or only a Frontline service offered.

Other churches have chosen to plant a new single generation church rather than seek to minister to that generation within their fellowship. In a sense, this is what First Baptist Church[5] in Rockwall, Texas, did when they planted our church in 1979. At that time they saw the suburbs of Dallas moving toward their county seat town and believed that rather than transforming what already existed, a new church could do a better job reaching the next generation.

For years Lake Pointe had the luxury of concerning itself with only one generation, the Boomers. As new generations came on the scene, we chose to slowly evolve musically rather than create a separate service, a church-within-a-church, or a new church plant. We chose that route for several reasons. First, there was less of a style difference between the Boomers, Busters, and subsequent generations, than there had been between the Builders and the Boomers. Second, many of the generational issues are addressed by our affinity-based, midsized, and small group matrix (Life Groups and Growth Groups addressed in a previous chapter).

However, by 2005, we had become a large enough church that even the very small percentage of Builders in our church had become a substantial number. I sensed that this group, while loving our church, was at best tolerating our worship style. So we announced that if 250 individuals would sign a commitment to attend a "classic (traditional) service," we would offer such a service in one of our larger classrooms. Enough people signed up and we held the first service. Four-hundred-sixty people showed up the first Sunday. The next week we moved the service to the gym.

This Classic Service continues to reach a niche in our community every Sunday. They watch a DVD of the sermon that is recorded the night before at our Saturday service. It is the same message all of our people hear each week. The difference is that before the message, they worship with a choir and orchestra and express their faith authentically with traditional hymns.

Of course, it is very easy to overgeneralize characteristics of each generation (e.g., not all Busters come from a broken home), and I believe to a large extent some Christian writers have contributed to the creation of differences rather than observing them (e.g., candles in worship). However, I believe there are some generational distinctives beyond merely music preferences and dress customs that are helpful to note and are generally true for most in a generation.

We should not be surprised that each generational tribe carries a different set of expectations with them when they walk into the doors of our churches. So how does a tribal leader navigate these different generational expectations?

Critical mass is one key in deciding whether or not to offer multiple formats to reach different generations. It can be expensive to provide a variety of styles, and the church needs to decide whether its current staff has both the ability, time, and money to pull it off. Also, each church needs to decide the extent to which separate services and/or programming divides the church and at what point it might become unhealthy or violate its own values or vision to separate the generations.

Make no mistake, it will take all kinds of churches of all sizes, strategies, and styles to reach our world for Christ.

	Traditionalists	Boomers	GenXers	Millenials
	(Born 1925–45)	(Born 1946–1964)	(Born 1965–1980)	(Born 1980–2000)
Driving Values	Respect authority, Delayed Gratification	Optimism, Involvement	Skepticism, Informality	Tolerance, Realism, Social
Family Dynamic	Traditional Nuclear	Disintegrating	First day care, latch-key	Blended families, Coddled kids
Communications	Formal memo, rotary phone	Touch-tone phone, call anytime	Cell Phone, e-mail	Texting, Social Networks
Money	Save, pay cash, tithe	Buy now, pay later	Save, spend cautiously	Earn to spend
Job is . . .	A duty	An identity	A contract	Means to an end
Leadership Style . . .	Command & control	Consensus, Collegial	Egalitarian, Ask "Why?"	Too soon to know
Interactive Style . . .	Individual	Team Meetings	Entrepreneur	Participative
Christian Music . . .	George Beverly Shay	The Imperials	Michael W. Smith	Chris Tomlin
Church Movement	Evangelicalism	Seeker/Purpose Driven	Emerging	Too soon to know

Some will do a better job reaching certain generational tribes than others. While it is understandable that each church wants to reach as many of those generations and subgroups as they can, it may be unrealistic to believe that any one church can relate to everyone. Just as individuals must discover what vital and unique role we play in the body of Christ, so must each church determine which tribe or tribes it can best reach and disciple.

Leading Small Action Plan

Get started applying the concepts explored in this chapter with your church by inviting your leadership team to discuss their answers to the following questions.

Generation Tribes

"AS IS" Reality

1. Which category best describes the present reality of your church strategy regarding navigating various generational expectations?

- **Category One:** We have an aging congregation in part because we have not transitioned toward the expectations and needs of younger generations.
- **Category Two:** We are a single-generation-focused church for the most part, primarily attracting and serving one dominant group.
- **Category Three:** We have a variety of generations and preferences due to generation-focused tribal

ministry strategies and/or leveraging an intergenerational model.

2. Which generational tribe would you call your primary target audience?

"COULD BE" Dreams

Come up with at least twenty ideas of things you could do in the future to better reach and serve your target generational tribe in areas such as music, facilities, service length/format, cultural expectations, etc.

"MIGHT BE" Prototype

Drawing from these ideas and gleaning from models at other churches, describe a strategy you believe would help you leverage the generational dynamics of your congregation for greater impact rather than unhealthy conflict.

"SHOULD BE" Priorities

1. In light of your resource and schedule realities, what obstacles do you see to implementation? How might you resolve them?

2. Which elements of the proposed prototype should be top priority for a Phase One initiative?

"WILL BE" Priorities

1. What is the single most important step to be taken during the next 120 days in order to move toward implementation?

2. Who is the lead person responsible for success?

3. What budget/resources will he/she have to accomplish the objectives?

To make it easy to go deeper on the themes of this chapter we have provided a free video overview. Invite your leaders to watch the corresponding segment and come to the next team meeting ready to discuss the "Leading Small Action Plan" questions. Access the video at: TribalChurchBook.com.

Chapter Eight

New Tribe Members

While attending a conference at Saddleback several years ago, I asked Rick Warren the secret to church growth. He responded, "That's the wrong question—all living organisms grow. The real question we should be asking is what we are doing that restricts our church's growth." In the book of Acts, it says that every day they were adding to their number those who were being saved. Those we add to our number are a part of the new member tribe; if they are not new to the faith, they are new to the unique culture of each church.

Every year at Lake Pointe Church, we passionately seek to increase the "new member" tribe. This tribe is far from monolithic. Some of them come to our church with absolutely no knowledge of the Bible and little, if any, church background. On the other end of the spectrum, there are those who come with an extensive church background, including post-graduate and theological degrees or even church staff experience. All come with a preconceived idea of what it means to be a member of Lake Pointe. Some of their thinking is accurate; some is not. Many times their understanding is incomplete. This incomplete vision is why we make orientation a requirement for all new members regardless of their background.

The process of assimilating a new tribe member begins when a person completes an application for membership. This can happen in one of several ways. In the foyers of all our campuses, we have a Hospitality Center, where one of the campus pastors is stationed after every service. The campus pastor is the consistent face that is recognized at each campus. When an individual is ready to join, he or she wants to approach a familiar face, someone that person feels he or she knows to some degree.

At our community campuses, it is their local campus pastor who teaches three or four times a year, oversees communion, baptisms, prayer, and is the live spokesman in almost all their services. At our original campus it is the lead pastor.

The Hospitality Center is strategically located in the main foyer of all campuses so that it is easily seen and accessed as the crowd leaves a service. The walls are made of glass so that everyone may look into the room—which removes some of the mystery of what goes on within and encourages those who pass to enter.

The campus pastor stands at the entrance of the Hospitality Center. Behind him is a coordinator, who listens as individuals approach the pastor. Based on the conversation, the coordinator summons the appropriate counselor who is standing nearby. Equipped counselors are available to meet a variety of needs. These needs include transfers of membership, counseling for various struggles such as addiction or marital difficulties, assistance with children, questions about becoming a Christian, and the desire for prayer due to an illness or other crises in their lives.

In the early days Lake Pointe held a regular "come to the front" invitation at the close of each service. It was a remnant of our Baptist heritage and, before that, the mourners' bench of the Second Great Awakening. This approach worked fine in a rural church where a large crowd was several hundred people and everyone seemed to know everyone else in the community. As America and the church grew and became more urban, communities became more anonymous in nature. Thus, the public invitation became more of a barrier than a vehicle for helping people connect with a fellowship.

For those of us who grew up accustomed to a public invitation as a means of expressing faith or joining a fellowship, it was difficult to let go of that tradition. What we called the "altar call" provided a source of great encouragement as we saw people responding to God moving in their lives and joining our church. However, the reality was that the nature of the public invitation in a larger, less familiar setting was actually inhibiting people with certain personality types from taking the next step in their spiritual pilgrimage.

So in the early 1990s we began offering two options in addition to the public invitation. One option was to meet the pastor at the front of the church immediately after the service. The other was to place a card in the offering plate requesting a personal visit with a pastor. The option to meet the pastor at the front required the individual to "swim upstream" at the close of the service and walk against the crowd exiting the auditorium. Although the card option was available, I believe few used it because the visible invitation was so compelling it dwarfed the card option in everyone's mind.

In 1996 we moved into a new building and took the opportunity to make a major change in how people could join the church. With the exception of a few times a year, we no longer offer a public come-to-the-front invitation. When we made the change, several things happened. First, there was a howl of protest from a small group who proclaimed that people should be willing "to profess Christ before men." We gently reminded them that the come-to-the-front invitation historically was a fairly recent church phenomenon and that baptism was the biblical means by which to make a public profession. Second, we immediately saw an unprecedented number of inquiries for membership and salvation. Today we still offer the option of placing a card in the offering plate to indicate a decision. We have also added the option of utilizing our Web site to indicate a desire to join. However, most decisions made—as well as most counseling and prayer—still take place in the Hospitality Center. We also offer a free, leather-bound study Bible in the Hospitality Center to anyone who does not own a Bible of any kind. The discussions with those responding to the Bible offer have been extremely constructive and have led people to join the church and make other key decisions.

It amazes me that a number of churches have seen the wisdom of discontinuing the more public come-down invitation but have not replaced it with an appropriately accessible alternative. Many churches offer classes or receptions to those who express an interest in membership. However, these options require the potential member to attend another meeting that may or may not be convenient, thereby unnecessarily creating a time and schedule barrier to the process. Some churches do not provide any clear path to make a spiritual decision or to assimilation into the local church body.

For a Hospitality Center to work well, it needs to be centrally located, clearly visible, easily accessible, and well-staffed. The center can be called a variety of names such as "The Hospitality Center," "Guest Central," or "Connection Point." Keep in mind the value: *clear over cute.*

Once a person comes to the center and receives counsel, that person is given the appropriate follow-up materials. This is another benefit to this approach versus the come-down invitation option. The center provides a calm and quiet environment where adequate time may be given to any counseling. The come-down invitation, on the other hand, rushes pastors to complete the process in time to present the decision to the congregation, all the while trying to compete with music being played in the background.

Those joining the church also receive information on other opportunities such as Life Groups, New Christian classes, baptism times, and they are informed about the required orientation for all new members.

New Member Workshop

The three-hour New Member Workshop at Lake Pointe is held once a month on Sunday evenings. New members are encouraged to attend as soon as possible. Over the years we have experimented with different times to offer this

workshop. At times the workshop has been held on consecutive Sunday mornings, before and after the service, and also
on four consecutive Wednesday nights. The trial and error
method has taught us that one long session on a Sunday evening makes it more likely that our new members will attend
and complete the entire course.

Before they attend, all new members are asked to
complete a questionnaire and bring it with them to the
workshop. On that form they are asked to disclose their
church background and involvement, if any, and to recount
their salvation experience in their own words. They are also
asked to indicate whether or not they have already engaged
in either a Life Group and/or found their place of service at
Lake Pointe.

When they arrive at the workshop, they are asked to
turn in their questionnaire and their picture is taken for our
Web-based database. They are then seated at round tables.
Later in the evening, they are accompanied by selected hosts
who, after reviewing their questionnaires, help them develop
a customized plan of next steps for their first year in our
fellowship.

The workshop begins with a short DVD of the history
and values of Lake Pointe, helping the participants begin to
get a sense of the church family they are joining. The next
forty-five-minute session is led by our teaching pastor, which
is followed by a session led by the lead pastor. I teach this
session myself in order to communicate the importance of
the workshop.[1]

A Fully-Developing Follower

During this teaching time, the participants are invited to become "fully-developing followers of Christ." By this, we mean they should commit to growing in multiple ways, which we refer to as the "5 Ws."

1. Worshipping God
2. Contributing to God's Work
3. Impacting God's World
4. Living by God's Word
5. Walking with God's people

We believe there are at least three ways in which a believer **worships** God. First is corporately. Hebrews 10:25 exhorts us to avoid forsaking the assembling of ourselves together. We encourage new members to attend church regularly and show up on time. Second, we are to worship privately, praying and studying God's Word personally. In relaying this information, we suggest a simple plan of personal worship, including Bible reading and prayer. Finally, we are to have a lifestyle of worship (Mic. 6:8).

We also believe there are three primary ways in which we can **contribute to God's work**. One is through our finances. Here we talk about taking the next step in moving up the generosity ladder. For some who have never given, the next step is to begin giving something. For others, it is moving toward percentage giving. For those who are already practicing tithing, it is to move to sacrificial and Spirit-led giving beyond 10 percent. What we make clear is that to join

Lake Pointe, they must commit to taking the next step on that generosity ladder.

We also explain the variety of funds to which they can contribute (General, Building, Compassion, and Missions) and the variety of methods (direct deposit, online, offering plate, and mail). All of our members receive monthly offering envelopes in the mail along with a postage-paid business reply envelope. The only exceptions are those who have indicated that they plan to give online. At Lake Pointe, giving online has grown to represent about 15 percent of total giving and is getting larger every year. I have found that the percentage of members who give online is higher in the younger demographic churches with whom I consult.

Another way to contribute is through serving. We inform our members that we do not want them to serve in many places, but rather to choose one or two key roles. We ask them to be proactive and not wait for someone to ask them to join a team. They are encouraged to visit our Volunteer Center at any one of our campuses or go online to view the serving opportunities. Then to contact the appropriate person to volunteer and receive training.

Finally, we believe in relational stewardship. As members get involved in a small group of believers—or in a Life Group—they put themselves in a place where they can be blessed and can be a blessing to others.

We believe we **impact God's world** through both our personal witness and involvement in missions. Each member is given an "impact card," on which they are asked to list three individuals whom they know are lost or unchurched. They are then asked to make a commitment to pray for those three individuals, watch for an opportunity to witness to them, and when interest is shown, to invite them to Lake Pointe. We ask them to carry the "impact card" with them or place it where they can view it on a regular basis, and then to replace the names as necessary when those for whom they are praying come to know Christ.

When I was growing up, I thought the choices related to missions involvement were to give to missions, pray for missions, or go on mission. I have since discovered it involves all the above rather than just one. It is not multiple choice. Lake Pointe currently has deep relationships with fifteen churches in nine countries including China, Russia, Ghana West Africa, South Africa, New Zealand, Mexico, Egypt, Iraq, and Nigeria. Over the past ten years, we have also started churches in New York, San Francisco, Portland, Tampa, Las Vegas, Fort Worth, Boston, Boca Raton, Fort Collins, Colorado, and Mansfield, Texas. We also have partnerships with several inner-city churches and ethnic ministries in Dallas, and we operate a mission center for the needy in our own city, Rockwall, Texas.

We do not expect every one of our members to be personally involved in an overseas or foreign ministry every year. However, with the variety of local, national, and foreign mission opportunities available, we do expect our members to be involved in missions somewhere every year.

We believe **living by God's Word** is more than just attending multiple Bible studies each week and getting all your eschatological charts in order. Rather, it is making all your key life decisions—including those about your ethics, finances, relationships and values—under the authority of God's Word alone. In order to live by God's Word, our people must know God's Word. We challenge them to be self-feeders, to study God's Word daily, and then live out what they are learning.

We believe that **walking with God's people** is more than attending regular worship gatherings. It is about doing life together, rejoicing with those who rejoice and weeping with those who weep, sharing all things in common, and sharing with those who may have need. It is about having "Paul and Timothy relationships" with appropriate transparency, authenticity, and accountability (2 Tim. 2:2). All our new members are required to commit to attend a Life Group, are encouraged to go further and also join the small home-based Growth Groups, and then to develop accountability relationships with members of that group.

Following the presentation, the new members are invited to ask any questions they would like of the lead pastor. Typically, questions include inquiries about our denominational affiliations, form of governance, and the status of my long-term commitment to remain as pastor.

After the Question-and-Answer session, which usually lasts about fifteen minutes, I talk to them about their commitment to become members. I often use the metaphor of a football game to describe what it means to be a member. An American football game was once described as "thousands of people in the stands in desperate need of exercise, watching 22 people on the field in desperate need of a rest."[2] To join the church means, among other things, to step out of the stands, no longer content with just being spectators, to become participants.

To join Lake Pointe, new members must be willing to make the following five written commitments:

1. To be involved in a Life Group
2. To financially support the ministries of Lake Pointe in a God-honoring manner
3. To use their abilities to serve in a ministry
4. To pray for and invite others to come hear about God's love
5. To establish a regular time of personal prayer and Bible study

We then introduce each individual or each couple to their host(s). They leave everything at their table while they go to the buffet line, taking only their signed five commitments with them.

I strategically place myself at the front of the food line and receive their signed commitments in my left hand, while shaking their right hand. (Some of you will remember this from graduation.) It is what we call the "magic moment," the point at which our hands touch and the commitment is exchanged. I warn them that for some it is a very emotional—even spiritual—moment; but for most it is a rather stoic experience.

It is, however, a very important transaction. It is a personal acknowledgement and agreement with the membership responsibilities at Lake Pointe. They are committing to a tribe, yes, but they are also joining a team—one with a purpose. Every healthy church they will ever join will expect these reasonable church disciplines from them. However, many of them do not make a clear request. We believe that a good understanding makes for a long friendship.

The next obvious question is "Do we throw people out of our tribe if they do not fully keep their commitments?" This is a question we studied long and hard before we decided the answer is "no." We have decided not to make keeping these commitments "a test of fellowship." However, we do—and on a regular basis—gently and corporately remind our members of the commitments they made when they joined.

As a way of reinforcing these values, every year during the month of January, we invite all of our members to recommit themselves to the same five disciplines in a public service. This recommitment is a spiritual exercise and not required for continuation of membership in the tribe.

When new members join your church, do they fully understand what it means to be a member of your unique tribe? How, and when, are you communicating those expectations?

Leading Small Action Plans

Get started applying the concepts explored in this chapter with your church by inviting your leadership team to discuss their answers to the following questions.

New Tribe Members

"AS IS" Reality

1. Which category best describes the present reality of your church strategy regarding assimilating new members into your tribe?

- **Category One:** We do not have a clear process for new member assimilation.
- **Category Two:** We make it easy for new people to join us, but do not really clarify our expectations of them.
- **Category Three:** We have a clear process that makes it easy for those interested to take next steps and clarifies expectations.

2. On the whole, what grade would you give your present member assimilation process?

"COULD BE" Dreams

Come up with at least twenty ideas of things you could do in the future to make it easy and more likely those interested in joining your tribe will . . .

- Take a simple next step
- Understand the church mission, vision, and ministry strategy
- Understand what is expected of them as good church members
- Make an initial commitment to fulfill those expectations
- Remain committed over the long haul

"MIGHT BE" Prototype

Drawing from these ideas and gleaning from models at other churches, describe a strategy you believe would help you increase the percentage of visitors who take steps to learn more, the percentage of active attendees who commit to membership, and the percentage of members who remain active contributors.

"SHOULD BE" Priorities

1. In light of your resource and schedule realities, what obstacles do you see to implementation? How might you resolve them?

2. Which elements of the proposed prototype should be top priority for a Phase One initiative?

"WILL BE" Priorities

1. What is the single most important step to be taken during the next 120 days in order to move toward implementation?

2. Who is the lead person responsible for success?

3. What budget/resources will he/she have to accomplish the objectives?

To make it easy to go deeper on the themes of this chapter we have provided a free video overview. Invite your leaders to watch the corresponding segment and come to the next team meeting ready to discuss the "Leading Small Action Plan" questions. Access the video at: TribalChurchBook.com.

Chapter Nine

Campus Tribes

About twelve years ago, one of our elders asked the question: "If we continue to grow at our current rate, when will we run out of facilities here in Rockwall?" The answer, for us, turned out to be ten years. The next logical question was: "What do we need to do today so that the shoe does not tell the foot how large it can be?" The answer to this question was not as easily discerned.

We believed that relocation was not a viable option. We already had so much money invested in our current facility and knew that the resale value on church property at best would be only 25 cents on the dollar. We first considered purchasing adjacent land, if and when it became available. At the time, there were—and still are—several thriving commercial enterprises on either side of our thirty-six-acre campus, so the prospects for buying land remains slim.

We then decided to add a parking deck with a capacity of approximately two hundred parking spaces. We will continue to add two hundred elevated parking spaces in the future each time we add a new building to our current facilities. We decided to provide this form of parking in stages because the cost for each elevated parking space currently costs around $10,000. When we eventually cover our entire current parking lot with a one-level deck, we will have added an additional two thousand spaces. A multilevel parking garage was ruled out because other churches that had built such a structure advised against it due to the amount of time it takes people to exit.

Third, we decided to move an additional two hundred and fifty people from our Sunday morning service to our Saturday night service. If we could shift that same number each year for the next ten years, it would make a huge difference on Sundays.

Fourth, we provided a shuttle service each Sunday morning from a nearby shopping center.

Finally, we explored the possibility of opening other campuses in distant communities where a substantial number of our members were living.

It was through this difficult decision-making process that we discovered one of the most strategic tribes in a local church, the campus tribe.

In 2004, when we began to consider a multicampus strategy, twelve hundred churches across the United States were already doing so. As strange as the multiple-campus idea sounded, many churches had already beta tested the concept for us. While our space needs were the initial reason for considering multiple campuses, a more compelling reason soon sold us on the concept.

We discovered that those church members who were driving anywhere from 12 to 20 minutes one way to get to our church were not doing a very effective job of inviting their unchurched friends, family, and coworkers to Lake Pointe. Relational evangelism is our primary strategy for reaching the lost, and the distance that some of our members lived from church was creating an obstacle to that highly held value.

The location of our first community campus in Mesquite was determined by deciphering where the greatest number of our long-distance driving members resided. We had already decided to open a campus in Mesquite when we discovered that a like-minded church in the area was seeking to relocate in that same area. So we decided to join forces.

Today that campus, which is twelve miles west of Rockwall, averages a thousand in attendance each week and reflects the ethnic diversity of that part of our region. Our second campus, which began a few years later and is twenty miles north of us in Garland, is also a product of a merger with another church. That campus also averages about a thousand each weekend. Last year about three hundred of our members accepted the challenge to start a new campus twenty miles south of Rockwall, in Forney.

We have had many other opportunities to merge with existing congregations but have declined to do so. Most declining churches are not willing to change what is necessary to become more effective.

Our community campus in Mesquite has an eight-hundred-seat auditorium in a building that was formerly a sporting goods store, which we purchased and remodeled.

At our community campus in Garland, we purchased twenty acres and built a thirty thousand square foot building with a five-hundred-seat auditorium where they now hold four services each weekend.

Our Forney campus currently meets in a high school, and we are in the process of purchasing land for a future building.

Our most unique campus existed long before the campuses we started to help alleviate our space problems. Over a decade ago, one of our church members, who is a furniture salesman, started visiting the Dawson State Prison in downtown Dallas. Soon after, he asked for and received permission to begin showing videos of our church services on Monday mornings to some of the male population in the prison. Today we hold two services for women and one service for men at the prison with approximately four hundred in total attendance each week.

The Dawson State Prison campus has its own Life Groups, its own worship guide, and holds baptism services once every quarter. When released, many of the inmates go to one of the halfway houses that we run and eventually end up at one of our other campuses.

Almost all of our campuses receive their teaching through either satellite transmission, or in the case of the prison, by DVD. The exception is our Hispanic service, which is held on the Rockwall campus. That campus pastor preaches in Spanish. We also have a campus at a nearby retirement community and a classic venue at our Rockwall campus in our gym.

We have discovered that there is a segment of the population in any community that will not tolerate teaching via video no matter how well it is done. My guess is that about 25 percent of any community falls into that category, although I am sure it is higher or lower depending on the given culture.

However, before coming to a neighborhood where we now have a campus, we only had the opportunity to touch about 10 percent of the population because of the distance to our main campus. After we opened a video venue campus there, that opportunity was multiplied at least sevenfold.

Those who are considering the video venue approach to multiple campuses would do well to purchase multiple cameras, the graphic generating packages and equipment, and the associated switching tools early in the process to allow their media team the time to learn how to effectively use them before launching a new campus. Utilizing image magnification at the original campus also helps the congregation acclimate to watching the message on a screen and, therefore, makes recruiting to the other campuses easier.

Every campus, with the exception of Dawson State Prison, has live music, although our worship team and I go to the prison a couple of times a year to conduct live services. Every campus, including the prison, has a campus pastor. The campus pastor teaches three or four times a year to emphasize values that need extra attention at that particular campus. We believe that leadership takes place through teaching, and, if the campus pastor taught on a regular basis, our campuses would not all have the same vision. The campus pastor needs to have the ability to communicate and to lead but will probably not have teaching as his primary passion or gifting.

One of the major decisions related to community campuses is that concerning supervision. Does all the supervision
come from the original campus (e.g., student minister in
Rockwall supervises student minister at the Forney Campus)?
Or does the supervision take place with the pastor at each
community campus supervising the staff at that campus?
We have tried it both ways and found both—for different
reasons—can be troublesome. What works best, however, is
when the campus pastor supervises those on his campus as
it is difficult to coach someone from a distance. The original
campus staff in specialized ministries, such as children's and
youth, plays the role of major influencers. Certain aspects of
the campus ministry—where it makes sense not to duplicate
work—remain centralized such as accounting, communications, and some aspects of production and worship planning.
For example, our worship leader at the original campus plans
the worship sets for all campuses, and his team does all the
musical arranging. These sets are then given to the campus
worship leaders, thus saving them a lot of redundant effort.
The campus worship leader then has the freedom to change
any part of the set based on the personnel available on the
campus or to better fit their tribe's unique culture. The curriculum for the student and children's ministries is provided
for all campuses from the original campus, but each campus
once again has the freedom to make any necessary changes
to fit their situation. All campus events such as camps and
retreats are also centralized.

There are some who are critical of the multicampus
approach. They ask: "Why not just plant churches in the
area?" While some of the campuses may one day become

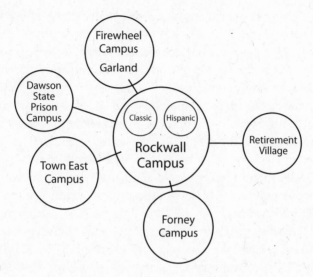

separate churches, the purpose of opening the campuses was to provide the Lake Pointe Church experience for those who were leaving their community and driving past other churches to attend Lake Pointe. Our goal was to get them to stay in their own community, to be salt and light there, and yet still provide them with a relationship with our church.

We now have a significant campus to the west, to the south, and to the north of our main campus as well as what I call *boutique* campuses at the prison and at the retirement community.

I do not foresee beginning any other major campuses in the near future since there is not significant population to the east of Rockwall. Our goal never was to extend our brand beyond our immediate region, and we believe that giving proper supervision and transferring DNA to extremely remote campuses is problematic at best.

Our purpose for our multicampus strategy remains to provide a better opportunity for our current membership to reach their community for Christ while providing space to grow at our main campus. A value added is that we are also able to better customize our ministries to those smaller campus tribes. Many churches may want to consider a multicampus strategy rather than the more costly option of a full relocation. It may provide another way of adding space incrementally without losing the original investment in a landlocked campus.

By going to the multicampus format, we are also able to benefit from the economy of volume. We are able to centralize certain functions of the church such as teaching, planning, and accounting, and thereby be better stewards by being more efficient.

We are also able to customize programming at each campus such as music styles, age group ministry, and specialized needs of the community in which they are located. These new campus tribes have also provided more opportunities for our people to serve and get involved.

These smaller campus tribes allow us to create a smaller, more personal environment for those who still want some of the opportunities a large church can provide. It is my hope that the story of our journey into a multicampus experience can open your eyes to some possible new solutions to your own challenges. The creation of campus tribes is an effective way of breaking a larger congregation into more manageable and localized tribes.

Leading Small Action Plan

Get started applying the concepts explored in this chapter with your church by inviting your leadership team to discuss their answers to the following questions

Campus Tribes

"AS IS" Reality

1. Which category best describes the present reality of your church with regard to expanding impact through multiple campuses?

- **Category One:** We have plenty of space right now and have never seriously considered an additional campus venue for our church. All of our current members live close enough to our campus to invite others.
- **Category Two:** We anticipate needing to explore additional space in the near future and/or have a critical mass of church members who live more than ten minutes away, and we are interested in the multi-campus concept.
- **Category Three:** We have multiple campuses now and intend to expand further in the future.

2. Summarize your current strategy for deciding when, where, and how to launch an additional campus venue.

"COULD BE" Dreams

Come up with at least twenty ideas of things you could do with multiple campuses that you can't do in one location.

"MIGHT BE" Prototype

Drawing from these ideas and gleaning from models at other churches, describe a strategy you believe would create the greatest possible facility capacity at the lowest possible cost.

"SHOULD BE" Priorities

1. In light of your resource and schedule realities, what obstacles do you see to implementation? How might you resolve them?

2. Which elements of the proposed strategy should be top priority for a Phase One initiative?

"WILL BE" Priorities

1. What is the single most important step to be taken during the next 120 days in order to move toward implementation?

2. Who is the lead person responsible for success?

3. What budget/resources will he/she have to accomplish the objectives?

To make it easy to go deeper on the themes of this chapter we have provided a free video overview. Invite your leaders to watch the corresponding segment and come to the next team meeting ready to discuss the "Leading Small Action Plan" questions. Access the video at: TribalChurchBook.com.

Chapter Ten

Planting New Tribes

It's embarrassing to say, but for many years, we did not spend much time thinking about missions. Sure, we gave to an annual missions offering, and when our student ministry became large enough, they started taking an annual summer mission trip—mostly to nearby Mexico.

Part of the problem, I think, was hidden in the fact that we were a church plant. We got stuck, especially in the early years, thinking of ourselves as being a mission rather than being on mission. We certainly had a burden for the lost in surrounding areas, but we did not have much of a vision beyond that. So during the first ten years, we gave to missions and even sent some of our families to plant two more churches in the nearby area, but we did not have a larger worldwide vision.

In 1996, while I was on a vision trip to mainland China, God gave our church a vision for the world. It was at that time that we realized we were being called as a church to make a greater difference in both our nation and in our world, which, among other things, included planting new tribes.

Making a Difference in Our World

Shortly after my vision trip to China, we began sending teams to speak in English classes in universities in Communist China. We also gave the necessary funds to construct a coffeehouse in one city, where new believers could connect with existing house churches. Over a period of time, we found there were more mission opportunities around the world presented to us than to which we could effectively respond. As a result, we determined that we would engage in mission work under the following guidelines.[1]

1. Lake Pointe's mission endeavors, with very few exceptions, will be church-to-church relationships.
2. Those churches must be ones with whom we have doctrinal and paradigm affinity. By paradigm affinity, we mean those who are willing to be aggressive and strategic in carrying out the Great Commission, giving equal emphasis to both evangelism and discipleship.
3. The churches with whom we partner need to be led by a pastor with teaching and leadership skills.
4. The partnership will be formalized only after a sufficient "dating period," which will include in-depth discussions and the sending of exploratory teams.

Lake Pointe currently has relationships with fifteen different churches in nine different countries. Last year Lake Pointe sent 967 individuals on short and midterm trips to those churches, and we currently have twenty-two church members working full-time in a variety of countries.

When Lake Pointe sends teams to any one of our mission partners, we want to make sure we are sending our best. With very few exceptions, we require that mission trip participants first be active in a Lake Pointe Life Group and be a financial contributor to the church. They are allowed to raise money from friends and family for the cost of the trip, but they must have at least 50 percent of their own money invested in a national or international trip. In addition to country-specific training, all participants must take an online personal evangelism-training course.

One of the by-products of our formal relationships with other churches around the world is that our members are beginning to think missionally. Many of them are now realizing that mission involvement is not limited to going on a church-sponsored trip to a church in another part of the world, but rather it is a way of life. As a church, we are seeing more and more of our people leverage their existing local, national, and international relationships in entrepreneurial ways to touch the world for Christ. The people of Lake Pointe are on mission around the world in more ways than we could possibly know about or control. We think this is a good thing.

Making a Difference in Our Nation

Lake Pointe also saw the need to begin planting churches in underchurched regions of the continental United States. Around the year 2000, I visited New York City and noticed a lack of conservative evangelical, new paradigm churches. We began praying for God to rise up a church planter to establish a church in New York that could serve as a model for effectively reaching that underresourced region for Christ.

In 2002 we joined an alliance of ten churches to provide the necessary funds to support Nelson Searcy in planting a church in Manhattan. All the churches involved committed to support the Manhattan church plant for a minimum of three years. Unlike some church planting networks, we would not decrease our support each year, but rather would keep it at the same level for the entire partnership.

The $250,000 we would provide together the first year would be 100 percent of the budget for the new church. The same amount would be 50 percent of their budget the second year, and then 25 percent of their budget the third and final year. As it turned out, most of the churches stayed at some level of support for a fourth year to give the church the ability to gradually wean off support. After going off support, the plants are encouraged to participate in future church planting initiatives.

Nelson Searcy and his wife, Kelly, had been in New York five days when the planes hit the World Trade Center towers. Although the September 11 tragedy dramatically changed our strategic plans for establishing that first national plant, we believed God's hand had sovereignly placed Nelson in New York City for the time of great spiritual hunger that followed.

After completion of the New York church plant, we took the lessons we learned and committed to planting a second New York City church, as well as one in Las Vegas, one in Tampa, Florida, and one in Portland, Oregon. The second wave of planting was followed by a third wave, in which we have planted, or are in the process of planting, three churches

in San Francisco, one in Boston, one in both Fort Worth and
Mansfield, Texas, and one in Fort Collins, Colorado. Our current capital campaign will provide $1 million of resources to
plant an additional seven churches over the next three years.

In addition to financial support, all churches in the
planting alliance also send teams to help the church launch.
Every year we send a survey to all our mission partners and
ask them the following questions:

- What type of skills do you need in our mission team
  members and what are the current projects in which
  you need their participation?
- What size team is best?
- What time of the year do you need a team?
- What were the "wins" of the last team we sent?
- How could we do a better job in serving you?

All of our teams bear their own expenses, including any
supplies for projects in which they are participating.

Here is what we have learned about national church
plants. First, the planter should have strong teaching skills
and be a strong leader. We use the D.I.S.C. personality
profile to get a degree of insight into how the potential
pastor is wired.[2] With very few exceptions, we have learned
that a D.I. profile is best for a planter, and second best in
our opinion is an I.D. profile. We have also used the Gallup
strengths referenced in Tom Rath's book *StrengthsFinder
2.0*, which measures natural strengths. Of the thirty-four
possible Gallup strengths, we found that a planter needs to
have at least two of what we would call "hard strengths."
Hard strengths would be one of the following:

Hard Strengths

- Maximizer—Possesses the ability to improve existing situations
- Strategic—Knows how to get there from here
- Competition—Strives to be the best at something
- Arranger—Moves components into their best role
- Command—Gives direction with clarity
- Activator—Gets things done
- Responsibility—Completes all assignments
- Woo—The extrovert who makes a positive impression
- Achiever—Always striving to give their best

If a planter has at least two hard strengths, the remaining combination of "soft strengths" do not seem to factor in determining success or failure. The following is a list of what we think are the Gallup soft strengths:[3]

Soft Strengths

Adaptability	Harmony
Analytical	Ideation
Belief	Includer
Communication	Individualization
Connectedness	Input
Consistency	Intellection
Context	Learner
Deliberative	Positivity
Developer	Relater
Discipline	Restorative
Empathy	Self-Assurance
Focus	Significance
Futuristic	

Second, the church planter needs to have strong teaching skills. The number of church planters supported by planting networks who have never heard them teach amazes me. This is a nonnegotiable ability for a church planter, and it is very easy to verify.

Third, the church planter should have some prior vocational experience and success in that field of endeavor. Prior work success tells you about the work ethic of the candidate and may also, depending on the nature of the previous job, give insight into what a person does well. People are not necessarily good at what they claim, but rather at what they have proven to do well. If you do not believe that, watch the early season episodes of *American Idol*.

A planter's previous vocational experience does not have to be in church-related work, although that would be preferable. In a perfect world, the planter would have prior experience in a successful existing church as a pastor or staff member.

Finally, and most importantly, a church planter needs to be a person of high character. There is obviously no inventory to measure this essential attribute, which is why it is important to know the candidate extremely well or know someone who does. The investment we make is too large to leave this issue to chance or to try to determine character with only interviews.

Other than the leader, we have found components to a strong plant are critical mass, team dynamics, location, and launch strategy. Many churches try to begin weekly services before they have a critical mass, which presents several problems. One issue resulting from starting weekly services too early is that the lack of a crowd communicates to the guests who attend a lack of success of the endeavor.

Another problem is that a small group causes the guests to feel exposed when most would rather remain anonymous. Lack of critical mass also puts a heavy burden on the young church to provide enough volunteers and financial resources to pull off quality weekend services.

One way to provide critical mass is to ask a sponsor church to send starter families. Another is to begin multiple Bible studies on different nights in various locations, which may later be combined once the church is launched. Critical mass can also be developed by recruiting Christians in the target area who have identified themselves in response to prelaunch mass communications.

One of the best books on church planting is *Launch* by Nelson Searcy and Kerrick Thomas.[4] Nelson recommends holding a series of monthly preview services for several months prior to the church holding weekly services. After each preview service, the pastor can contact those who attended and then use the time between services to recruit attendees to join the launch team. The time can also be used to plan and to advertise the next preview service.

Many new church plants are now being started by teams rather than by lone individuals. This strengthens the effort because more people are able to develop relationships in the target area, and the logistical burdens do not fall on one person with a narrow range of gifting. *Exponential* by Dave and Jon Ferguson[5] is a great resource on reproducing leaders to plant new campuses and churches.

The benefits of a church planter having a team with which to work requires more funding up front by supporting churches and/or means that some staff will be volunteers, bivocational, or initially raise their own support.

One of the lessons we learned in our New York church plant is how important the location can be. In New York City, being near a subway line is a factor in how many people see your church as a viable option. Obviously the plant needs to begin in the target area and be relatively easy for guests to find.

In a church plant's early days, people are more tolerant of a temporary venue, such as a school or theater, as long as it communicates the value of excellence as defined by the community.

With very few exceptions, excellent programming for children is also a key factor in success. The greatest growth engine for most church starts is families who are interested in church because they are beginning to have children.

A long-term strategy for any church must also include quality services with clear, relevant, biblically based messages, authentic worship music, and small groups that are easy to join. These small groups provide a place where care, interactive Bible study, involvement opportunities, and accountability can take place. Church plants without a strong small groups component usually remain as the small group themselves.

If the services are not practical and excellent, most members will not invite others. If the small Life Group tribes do not disciple those who are being reached, the back door will be wide open. In other words, the new tribe can only become a larger collection of tribes, in which newcomers feel welcomed, if the smaller tribes are doing their job of caring for individuals. To have a large impact, the church must continue to lead small.

We understand that there are many effective ways to plant new churches and ours is only one. We have chosen our particular strategy at this time because we believe it is important to establish strong larger regional churches in underresourced areas, which can then serve as a base of coaching and support to plant other indigenous churches in the same region.

Leading Small Action Plan

Get started applying the concepts explored in this chapter with your church by inviting your leadership team to discuss their answers to the following questions.

Planting New Tribes

"AS IS" Reality

1. Which category best describes the present reality of your church with regard to launching new tribes?

- **Category One:** We still see ourselves as a mission rather than on mission.
- **Category Two:** We have a missions program, but it has not been a major strategic priority for the church.

- **Category Three:** We have an aggressive church planting and/or missions strategy for regional and global
impact.

2. Summarize your process for deciding with whom you
will and will not partner when it comes to church plants or
missions.

"COULD BE" Dreams

Come up with at least twenty ideas of things you could
do in the future to exponentially expand your global impact
through church planting and/or global mission partnerships.

"MIGHT BE" Prototype

Drawing from these ideas and gleaning from models at
other churches, describe a strategy you believe would help
you increase the impact of your church throughout your
region and around the world.

"SHOULD BE" Priorities

1. In light of your resource and schedule realities, what
obstacles do you see to implementation? How might you
resolve them?

2. Which elements of the proposed prototype should be
top priority for a Phase One initiative?

"WILL BE" Priorities

1. What is the single most important step to be
taken during the next 120 days in order to move toward
implementation?

2. Who is the lead person responsible for success?

3. What budget/resources will he/she have to accomplish the objectives?

To make it easy to go deeper on the themes of this chapter we have provided a free video overview. Invite your leaders to watch the corresponding segment and come to the next team meeting ready to discuss the "Leading Small Action Plan" questions. Access the video at: TribalChurchBook.com.

Chapter Eleven

The Unreached Tribe

In his book, *Seven Strategy Questions*, Harvard Business School professor Robert Simons says: "Customers rightfully expect undivided attention and resources of businesses that compete to serve their needs. So it is vitally important to be clear about who is—and who is not—a customer."[1] Obviously, Simons is saying that one of the critical questions that must be answered by any enterprise is "Who is our customer?" For the church, our customers are in one of two groups:

1. Believers we are seeking to disciple.
2. Those who have not yet become Christians.

Since Lake Pointe began, we have gone to great lengths to keep both tribes in mind as we have made our strategic plans. Churches have a tendency to lean toward only one of these two tribes. We all know churches that emphasize evangelism so much that they may baptize scores of people every year but never increase in attendance. This is because they have not done an adequate job of caring for and developing the new believer tribe.

On the other hand, there are churches that circle the wagons and become a kind of fortress unaware, afraid of or just unconcerned about a lost world just outside of their Christian ghetto. Neither alternative is acceptable, if we are going to take seriously the Great Commission.

From time to time I like to ask our congregation, "When you fly in an airplane, would you rather have a right wing or a left wing?" The church cannot choose between evangelism and discipleship any more than a plane can rely on one wing or the other. Both are essential.

We have already talked about Life Group tribes, which I believe is the best vehicle for discipleship. This chapter is about the evangelism side of that equation. Lake Pointe has chosen relational evangelism as our primary strategy to reach those who have yet to join our tribe. We do not believe the most effective method for reaching the lost is to program events and expect lost people to come to us. There is no command in the Bible for lost people to come to church. There is a command for Christians to go to lost people (see Acts 1:8).

We also believe it is best—in almost all situations—for our people to share their faith in the context of their existing relationships, rather than to share with strangers. Without question, you will find examples in the Bible of what I call "guerrilla evangelism." This is where a believer strikes up a conversation with a total stranger, like Philip did when, led by the Spirit, he shared with the Ethiopian eunuch. I believe those individuals who have the spiritual gift of evangelism have the unique ability to share their faith effectively with strangers. Most of our people, however, have not been given that gift. These people will be more effective sharing their faith with those who they already know.

In Acts 10, Peter witnesses to Cornelius, and it says he and his whole "household" were converted. The Greek word *oikos* is used throughout the New Testament to describe one's "household." We all have an oikos, a network of existing relationships with whom we can share Christ. Every week thousands of our people are interacting with the unchurched in their day-to-day life. Rather than pressure our people to come to the church on a Tuesday night to be sent out to talk to total strangers, we encourage our people to share the gospel with the unbelievers they already know.

The goal of our churches should be to mobilize 100 percent of our believers for evangelism. This is severely hindered, if we limit our understanding of evangelism to include only those whose personality types and spiritual gifts allow them to share Christ "cold turkey" with strangers. This is why we ask all of our new members to make a commitment to pray for three people they already know and to seek to witness to them, and, when they show interest, to invite them to Lake Pointe.

We see evangelism as a team sport. Every team member just needs to play his or her role. The Bible says that one plants, another waters, and God gives the increase. Every member may not be called upon to close the sale. Their job is just to help those they already know to take one step closer to faith.

One key element in this process is to have a weekend service to which your church members are not embarrassed to invite unchurched friends. This does not mean that all your services must be evangelistic or geared only toward unbelievers. However, it does mean that you are aware that lost people may be present in any service and program and communicate accordingly.

A helpful metaphor is that of a family meal where an invited guest is present. Healthy, nourishing food would still be served to your own family to help them grow. However, with a guest present, you would not tell private jokes, discipline your children, or talk about details of family finances. You would take pains to explain some of the dishes served that are common to your family but may be new to your guest. Hopefully, by the time the meal was over, your guest would think, "Wow, I wish I could be a part of a family like this with a faithful father (God) who provides for His children like that."

When we look at programming or events for our church, we always ask the question, "Who is this for?" We believe there are four levels to consider when planning programming, events, or services.

Level 0—Pre-evangelism: The gospel is not necessarily shared at this event. It is an opportunity for our people to rub shoulders with the nonchurched at events held on or off our property such as a Fall Festival for families, or at a community service project like building a Habitat for Humanity home.

Level 1—For the Curious: This event or programming is specifically aimed for the non-believer. The gospel will be shared in a clear way and some type of opportunity to respond will usually be given.

Level 2—For the Convinced: This activity is geared toward those who are already saved. An example of this would be one of our weekly Life Group meetings. It is assumed that everyone who attends this Level 2 activity is already a believer; thus, we are able to go deeper and talk about issues that we might not deal with at a Level 1 activity. By the way, we do not believe that Life Groups are the best vehicle for evangelism. With very few exceptions, we do not believe that lost people want to attend a Bible study with a small group of Christians who have been studying the Bible together for several years.

Level 3—For the Contagious Contributor: This is an activity for believers who are committed to the purpose of the church. An example of this is leadership training.

The reality is that a typical weekend service is both a Level 1 and Level 2 event. It is the best place to do evangelism and yet cannot be given exclusively to that task because it is also the time when many Christians who are not yet connected to Life Groups attend.

Although we want our people to invite their lost friends on any weekend, we do declare some as "Impact Weekends." These are weekends specifically designed to share the gospel. Our intent is to give our people a heads-up and lead time to get their friends to these services. Several weeks prior, we announce the topic for an impact service and provide special "invite" cards for them to distribute, which include service times and maps.

Since relational evangelism is our primary strategy for winning new tribe members, it is important that we encourage our people to develop relationships outside the church.

This is more difficult for some of our members than for others. Some of our members have plenty of contact with the lost. Many have family members and friends who have not yet come to faith. They just need to become sensitive to the opportunities to influence those already in their daily lives.

Other people in our church need to restructure their daily paths to allow them to be around the unchurched more. Some have been believers so long that all of their time is spent at church or with Christian friends. John 4 states that Jesus went out of the common travel patterns of Jews of that day to go to the Samaritan village of Sychar. At Sychar, He encountered the Samaritan woman who was searching for meaning in her life. In the same way, some of our people need to change their daily path or become sensitized to those already in their path who have not found Christit. We as church leaders make a transition to that mind-set very difficult if we overprogram at the church, making it more difficult for our people to find time to develop relationships outside the church.

As a church gets bigger, it is important for leaders to keep their eyes on a few key numbers to determine how well they are doing in both evangelism and discipleship. Those statistics become a dashboard of the vibrancy and effectiveness of the organization. Lake Pointe's dashboard has nine primary numbers, which fall into four categories:

Conversions
- Number of baptisms
- Number completing New Member Workshop

Crowd
- Number attending worship

Community
- Number attending weekly Life Groups (midsized on-site groups)
- Number involved in Growth Groups (monthly home-based groups of 8 to 10 participants)
- Number of accountability partners (1 to 3 same-gender participants who meet together on a regular basis)

Committed[2]
- Percentage Total Number of Givers—divided into four categories:
  - Gave nothing in 12 months.
  - Gave $1 to $1,800 in 12 months, which is a tithe on a poverty level income for a family of 3 in the U.S.
  - Gave more than poverty level but less than a tithe.
  - Gave a tithe or more.
- Percentage and Total Number Serving in a Ministry
- Percentage and Total Involved in Mission

The first category of the "conversions" consisting of the number of baptisms and the number of those completing the New Member Workshop is the early indicator of the church's health.

I have found that our members are willing to do almost anything before they are willing to share their faith. The fires of personal evangelism are the first ones to go out in a church. As leaders, we must continue to stoke that fire by inviting every member to participate, by providing lifestyle evangelism training for our people, by holding up heroes who share their faith, and by modeling relational evangelism ourselves.

In Acts 2, it says that the early church was adding to its tribe those who were being saved every day. New tribe members are a sign of a healthy tribe.

Leading Small Action Plan

Get started applying the concepts explored in this chapter to your church by inviting your leadership team to discuss their answers to the following questions.

The Unreached Tribe

"AS IS" Reality

1. Which category best describes the present reality of your church with regard to reaching unbelievers in your community?

- **Category One:** We have experienced very little growth from evangelism in recent years beyond the direct activities of the pastoral team.

- **Category Two:** Our people invite others to church, but they seem hesitant or nervous about sharing the gospel themselves.
- **Category Three:** We have a process that makes it easy for those who might not have the gift of evangelism to invite others and share the faith in the natural context of existing relationships.

2. Summarize your current strategy for emphasizing evangelism and equipping your people to invite others and share the gospel.

"COULD BE" Dreams

Come up with at least twenty ideas of things you could do in the future to make it easy and more likely those who attend your church will reach unbelievers.

"MIGHT BE" Prototype

Drawing from these ideas and gleaning from models at other churches, describe a strategy you believe would help you increase the evangelistic temperature of your church.

"SHOULD BE" Priorities

1. In light of your resource and schedule realities, what obstacles do you see to implementation? How might you resolve them?

2. Which elements of the proposed prototype should be top priority for a phase one initiative?

"WILL BE" Priorities

1. What is the single most important step to be taken during the next 120 days in order to move toward implementation?

2. Who is the lead person responsible for success?

3. What budget/resources will he/she have to accomplish the objectives?

To make it easy to go deeper on the themes of this chapter we have provided a free video overview. Invite your leaders to watch the corresponding segment and come to the next team meeting ready to discuss the "Leading Small Action Plan" questions. Access the video at: TribalChurchBook.com.

Two words of caution to those who hope to become an effective tribal church leader.

First, avoid becoming defensive when you work through strategic questions with your team. This is especially difficult if you are the founding leader or if the present reality developed under your guidance. Humble leaders hold the past loosely in order to move toward a better future.

Second, keep in mind that the ideas in this book are designed to provide a helpful framework for gradual, ongoing progress. Do not try to move aggressively on all fronts at the same time or you undermine the power of leading small.

One step at a time.

Little by little.

Walk before you run.

In other words, be faithful in the little things and let God bring the big impact.

Conclusion

Several years ago the Willow Creek Association created *Reveal,* a tool for surfacing tribes that exist within every congregation who are at different levels of spiritual development. Their breakdown included those "exploring Christ," those "growing in Christ," those who are identified as "close to Christ," and the most mature group, "Christ-centered."[1] Identifying and tracking the progression of these tribes toward deeper engagement with Christ and His church allows leaders to create unique strategies for each tribe. This makes it more likely that every tribe member will move toward greater spiritual maturity.

If you do not understand the tribal nature of your church, your effectiveness will be hindered greatly. That's what this book has been about. The list of tribes we have highlighted includes individual families, small groups, church leadership, boards, different generations, new members, separate campuses, new churches, and the unreached of your community. This list of tribes is certainly not exhaustive, but it is a significant starting point. I encourage you to gather your team for a brainstorming session and see how many tribes you can identify within your own congregation and surrounding community. Each tribe that surfaces in your discussion will demand its own strategy and require your leaders to learn to speak new languages in order to relate to them.

To what extent do the communicators on your team understand the different ways the male and female tribes in their audience process information? How can social media be used to relate to, encourage, and customize communication to each tribe that exists in your congregation? How might an Internet campus minister to existing tribes that cannot or will not currently visit your bricks-and-mortar campus? How might an Internet campus even create new tribes?

These and many other pertinent questions must be addressed if we are to live out the value that the apostle Paul described when he said in 1 Corinthians 9:22, "I have become all things to all people, so that I may by all means save some."

When Paul says in 1 Thessalonians 5:14, "And we exhort you, brothers: warn those who are lazy, comfort the discouraged, help the weak, be patient with everyone," he reminds us that one size does not fit all. Different tribes require different communications, unique approaches, and customized strategies.

Many times when I ask local church leaders, "Who is your target audience?" they respond, "We want to reach everyone." While that lofty aspiration is admirable, the extent to which that goal becomes a reality in local churches depends upon their awareness of, and their efforts to creatively relate to, the many tribes that make up any community and every church.

Appendix A

Home Tribe Realities

You have probably heard the statistics. For more than a decade, church leaders have been bombarded by one report after another suggesting churched kids are rejecting Christian faith at an alarming rate. Unfortunately some widely quoted reports lack statistical veracity because there have been few longitudinal studies of generational faith transference. We also lack historical data for comparison. We have given up trying to pinpoint a precise statistic since each report seems to ask a slightly different question or explore the problem from a different angle. However, the collective data strongly suggests that about half of those raised in church back away from active faith as adults. And the problem is not at church but rather at home. Consider the following . . .

Declining Christian Affiliation: According to a 2001 study conducted by the Graduate Center of City University of New York, large numbers of American adults are disaffiliating themselves from Christianity.[1] U.S. polling data from the study indicates that of those who identify themselves with a specific religion, only 76.5 percent identified themselves as

Christian—a drop of nearly 10 percent in one decade. This decline matches trends observed in Canada between 1981 and 2001. If the trend continues, Christianity will become a minority religion in the U.S. by the year 2042.[2]

The End of Christian America: Research summarized in the 2007 book titled *unChristian: What a New Generation Really Thinks About Christianity* by David Kinnaman and Gabe Lyons[3] showed that the increasingly negative perception of the Christian faith has been fueled by the fact most of those who consider themselves unchristian in America are actually former church kids. As the book explains, "This leads to the sobering finding that the vast majority of outsiders in this country, particularly among young generations, are actually de-churched individuals."[4]

Losing Our Teens?: In October of 2006 the *New York Times* ran a cover story with the headline, "Fearing Loss of Teenagers, Evangelicals Turn up the Fire." The writer reported that, "Despite their packed megachurches . . . evangelical Christian leaders are warning one another that their teenagers are abandoning the faith in droves." The paper publicized a movement that has been growing to reinvest in young believers to stem an often-repeated warning that only a small portion of today's teen evangelicals will hold onto their faith as adults. The increased media attention is putting the problem of generational faith transference in the spotlight and raising interest in effective responses.

College Not the Problem: Contrary to popular opinion, college is not the problem. In fact, a slightly higher percentage of emerging adults who do not attend college drop out of religion than those who do attend college.

> One recent study, for instance, using some of the best longitudinal data available, has shown that it is not those who attend college but in fact those who do not attend college who are the most likely to experience declines in religious service attendance, self-reported importance of religion, and religious affiliation. Another showed that among recently surveyed college students, 2.7 times more report that their religious beliefs have strengthened during their college experience than say their beliefs weakened. . . . In every case, emerging adults currently in college are slightly more religious than those who are not in college.[5]

Student Ministries Not the Problem: Some have pointed the finger of blame at age-graded student ministry in churches. But James Shields begs to differ based upon a 2008 survey of several hundred young adults who had been active in a megachurch student ministry as teens and remained somewhat active. Most claim to have continued attending church on a fairly regular basis, although less than while living at home.[6]

Age of Conversion: About 65 percent of those who become believers in Jesus Christ do so as minors.[7] Children ages 5 to 13 have a 32 percent probability of coming to Christ. Those in and beyond their teens have a 4 to 5 percent probability.[8] This observation was reinforced by a separate study conducted by a University of Notre Dame team. Nearly one-third of emerging adults surveyed by the Center for the Study of Religion and Society made NO religious commitment by age twenty-three.[9] The vast majority of those who had made a commitment to live their lives for God appear to have made their first commitment well before the age of fourteen.

> These findings complement and reinforce one
> of the larger stories of this book: that the religious
> commitments and orientations of most people
> appear to be set early in life and very likely follow
> a consistent trajectory from that early formation
> through the adolescent and into the emerging
> adult years. Most are set early in life to follow one
> religious trajectory or another—mostly, we showed
> earlier, formed by the religious lives of their
> parents.[10]

Faith Commitment Timing:

- No Faith Commitment: 31%
- Committed Before Age Fourteen: 59%
- New Teen Commitments: 5%
- Emerging Adult Commitments: 5%

Faith Retention Rates: The same study revealed that 17 percent of emerging adults become more religiously active than they were during high school while 55 percent back away from active faith. Among those who continue to associate with a childhood tradition, some groups show higher retention rates than others.[11]

- Latter-Day Saints: 72% Retained
- Nonreligious: 68%
- Roman Catholic: 66%
- Conservative Protestant: 64%
- Jewish: 61%
- Other Religions: 60%
- Black Protestant: 55%
- Mainline Protestant: 50%

Marriage, Parenthood, and Faith: The 2009 book *Souls in Transition* summarizes a longitudinal study of "emerging adults" ages 18 to 23 conducted by the Center for the Study of Religion and Society at the University of Notre Dame. They found that,

> Marriage, children and religion tend to go together, at least in the United States. So the more marriage and children are delayed, the more religious involvement is postponed and perhaps never reengaged (if ever engaged in the first place). One of the strongest factors that brings young adult Americans back to religion after a probable hiatus during emerging adulthood is their formation of new families and especially having children. In the causally reverse direction, being more religious also makes people more likely to marry at all, to marry earlier, to have children at all, and to bear them at a younger age—thus, the strong family/religion connection in the United States is mutually reinforcing, even synergistic. All else

being equal, then, we can say that the younger
Americans are when they marry and bear children, the more religious they are likely to be. So
the postponement of settling down that is associated with emerging adulthood unintentionally
produces, as a causal mechanism, the tendency for
Americans to reduce religious involvements during
this phase of life.[12]

Leaving and Returning: The Southern Baptist Convention
(SBC) is America's largest Protestant denomination. In
recent years, conflicting statistics have surfaced about generational faith transference—the most dramatic claiming
94 percent of kids abandon the church after graduating from
high school. As many expected, that claim proved an exag-
geration. Authors Thom and Sam Rainer conducted research
among Southern Baptist young adults[13] that revealed that
about 70 percent drop out between the ages of eighteen and
twenty-two.[14] The vast majority stopped attending church
due to a change such as moving away from home, attending
college, or starting a career. The good news is that about two-
thirds of the 70 percent who drop out come back, although
their attendance is much less regular. What brought them
back to church? The most common reasons given, not sur-
prisingly, were "getting married" and "having children." The
30 percent who did not drop out of church were much more
likely to grow up in a home with parents who remained
married to one another, gave their children direct spiritual
guidance, discussed spiritual matters and/or prayed with
them. Most of those who remained active attended church

with their parents. Most of those who dropped out went to a different church than their parents. In short, they attended church when young with their parents and came back with a spouse and children of their own. Clearly, marriage and parenthood serve as the glue connecting us to active faith.

Historic Trends: In a recent *Policy Review* essay "How the West Really Lost God," Hoover Institute's Mary Eberstadt demonstrates how a society that moves away from the priority of family drives itself further from God. "Something about the family inclines people toward religiosity." She shows that in Western Europe unprecedented family shrinkage (decline in marriage, parenthood) appeared sometimes before and sometimes in tandem with the unprecedented decline in belief. In light of historical precedence, Eberstadt suggests, motherhood and fatherhood strengthen spiritual commitment because they are "the human symphony through which God has historically been heard by many people" and that family and children are the means "through which people derive their deepest opinions and impressions of life."[15]

Decline in Parenthood: A 2006 report called "Life Without Children" examines how a delay in parenting, decline in births, and devaluing of parenthood is making America less child-centered. It states,

> We are in the midst of a profound change
> in American life. Demographically, socially and
> culturally, the nation is shifting from a society of
> child-rearing families to a society of child-free

adults. The percentage of households with children has declined from half of all households in 1960 to less than one-third today—the lowest percentage in the nation's history. Indeed, if the twentieth century aspired to become the "century of the child," the twenty-first may well become the century of the child-free. . . . It is hard enough to rear children in a society that is organized to support that essential social task. Consider how much more difficult it becomes when a society is indifferent at best, and hostile at worst, to those who are caring for the next generation.[16]

What Fueled "Seeker" Movement? To some degree the Church Growth Movement of the past few decades helped slow the decline of Christian faith in America. Once again, however, that movement's engine was family formation. "Churches are full of people who left church as single, young adults and returned to the pews when they had families of their own," writes religion reporter Paul Asay.[17] Why? University of Chicago professor Dr. Leon Kass said it like this: "It is fatherhood and motherhood that teach most of us what it took to bring us into our own adulthood. And it is the desire to give not only life but a good way of life to our children that opens us toward a serious concern for the true, the good, and even the holy. Parental love of children leads once wayward sheep back into the fold of church."[18]

Toward a "Sticky" Faith

Even the most conservative reports suggest that Christianity has become less "sticky" than it was in past generations. And the reason, in our view, is because we have been neglecting the primary engines of lifelong faith, marriage, and parenthood.

This is why we invested two years facilitating dialogue with a network of innovative pastors who agree that the home must become a key strategic priority for the local church. The Strong Families Innovation Alliance included leaders from some of the nation's most respected churches including Willow Creek Community, Saddleback, Lakewood Church, Lake Pointe Church, Scottsdale Bible Church, and about a dozen other congregations of various sizes and traditions. We invited the full range of pastoral perspectives including senior and executive pastors, teaching and small group pastors, spiritual formation and discipleship pastors, as well as student and children's pastors. This group of leaders cooperated together to clarify goals, identify challenges, and develop workable strategies helping the church inspire family intentionality. We hope your church will join the movement in order to better equip the most important tribes in your congregation.

Learn more at

DriveFaithHome.com

Appendix B

Lake Pointe Church Policies Governing the Board

(The Board's Function)

Board Job Description

The purpose of the board, on behalf of the congregation, is to see to it that the church (1) achieves its mission and (2) observes biblical standards. The specific job of the board is to ensure the implementation of its primary and occasional responsibilities, which include but are not limited to the following:

Primary responsibilities

1. The board will pray for the congregation, the pastoral staff, and themselves.
2. The board will oversee the church's spiritual condition.
3. The board will produce and authorize overall written church policy in four areas.

   • The policies governing the board itself.

- The policies governing the Lead Pastor.
- The policies governing the board's relationship to the Lead Pastor.
- The policies reflecting the church's theology and practices.

4. The board will provide supervision of, accountability for, and protection of the Lead Pastor.
5. The board is responsible for overseeing recommendations regarding church discipline.
6. The board is responsible for doctrinal clarification.
7. The board is responsible for approving the licensing and ordination of individuals to the Gospel Ministry.

Occasional responsibilities

8. The board will oversee the selection process of the Lead Pastor.
9. The board will serve as an arbitrator in any disputes with the Lead Pastor.
10. The board will enforce policy relative to board members' attendance, preparation, policy-making principles, respect of roles, and ensuring continuance of leadership capability.
11. The board will continually work on its development, including orientation of new board members in the board's governance process, periodic discussion of process improvement, and continuous education of board members.
12. The board is responsible for establishing fair compensation and benefits for the Lead Pastor according to his

training, prior experience, size of church, tenure, and productivity.

Leadership Style

The board will lead with an emphasis on strategically accomplishing the church's stated purpose, including: (1) evangelism and discipleship, (2) encouragement of different viewpoints, (3) leadership rather than administrative detail, (4) clear distinction of board and Lead Pastor roles, (5) collective rather than individual decisions, (6) future focus rather than past or present, and (7) proactivity rather than reactivity, passivity, or negativity.

Chairperson's Role

The board's chairperson will assure the integrity and fulfillment of the board's process and, when necessary, may represent the board to the congregation and to outside parties. The job of the chairperson is to see that the board behaves consistently within its own rules and those legitimately imposed upon it from outside the organization. Accordingly,

1. Deliberation will be fair, open, and thorough but also timely, orderly, and to the point.
2. The chairperson is empowered to chair board meetings with all the commonly accepted power of that position (for example: ruling, recognizing).
3. The chairperson may represent the board to outside parties in announcing board-stated positions and in stat-

ing chair decisions and interpretations within the area delegated to him.

4. In such cases where the chairperson is not the Lead Pastor, he has no authority to supervise and direct the Lead Pastor.

Board Member's Qualifications

Board members must meet the biblical and other prudent qualifications for board membership (1 Tim. 3:1-7; 2 Tim. 2:2; 2:22; Titus 1:5–9).

1. Board members should be reliable (trustworthy) and teachable men who must meet spiritual leadership qualifications.
2. They should have sufficient tenure in the church to have proven themselves to be fully developing followers of Christ.
3. They need to agree with the church's core values, mission, vision, strategy, and doctrine.
4. Though they're not to be "yes" men, they do need to be loyal to the Lead Pastor and his leadership.
5. They must be members that are involved in the ministry of the church.
6. Their spouses must be supportive of their service on the board.

Board Member's Code of Conduct

The board commits itself and its members to ethical, biblical conduct, including proper use of authority and appropriate decorum when acting as board members. Accordingly,

1. Board members must work together as a unified team in the best interests of the entire church.
2. They must be courageous and make the right decisions no matter how unpopular or controversial.
3. They must trust and respect one another.
4. They must deal well with disagreements among themselves.
5. They must care about, genuinely appreciate, and most importantly respect and trust one another (this includes the Lead Pastor).
6. They must not be preservers of the status quo or tradition but open to new ways of doing ministry.
7. They must commit to attend the meetings of the board.
8. They may not attempt to exercise individual authority over the organization except as explicitly set forth in board policies.

   - Board members have authority over others (other board members, Lead Pastor, staff, congregation) only when acting *corporately* as a board.
   - They must not attempt to exercise *individual* authority over others in the church (other board members, Lead Pastor, staff, congregation).

9. Their individual interaction with the public, press, congregation, or others must not attempt to speak for the board except to repeat explicitly stated board decisions.
10. They will give no consequence to nor voice criticism of the Lead Pastor or staff performance beyond the board.
11. They will respect the confidentiality appropriate to issues of a sensitive nature.
12. They must avoid conflict of interest with respect to their board member responsibilities.
13. They will not corporately or individually interfere with the staff in its ministry.
14. Members, when serving in staff-directed ministries, will be under the direct authority of that staff person and the indirect authority of the pastor.

Board Member's Operations

The board commits itself to operate biblically and efficiently in conducting its meetings, making the best use of its time. Accordingly,

1. The board will make its decisions by consensus, defined as a simple majority vote. The final decision will be the position of the board (as if there was no difference of opinion).
2. The election and term of board members should comply with the church's Bylaws and Constitution.

Evaluation of Board Members

On an annual basis, the board will evaluate itself in written form corporately. Additionally, each board member will conduct a self-evaluation.

Policies Governing the Lead Pastor

(The Lead Pastor's Function)

Pastor's Job Description

The Lead Pastor oversees the general spiritual condition of the church and leads its operational ministry, including all staff.

1. The Lead Pastor is to protect the congregation from false teaching (Acts 20:28).
2. The Lead Pastor will preach and teach the Bible (1 Tim. 5:17).
3. The Lead Pastor is to lead or direct the affairs of the church (1 Tim. 5:17).

   - Pursues the church's mission and casts its vision (Matt. 28:19–20)
   - Develops and implements the church's strategy

- Identifies the church's community for outreach.
- Develops a disciple-making process.
- Leads the church's staff.
- Assesses the church's location and facilities
- Oversees the church's finances
- Establishes culturally relevant evangelistic ministries to reach lost people
- Establishes edifying ministries that move saved people toward spiritual maturity as well as address their spiritual needs

4. The Lead Pastor (not the board) is ultimately responsible for the recruitment, hiring/enlistment, and dismissal of all paid and unpaid staff.
5. The Lead Pastor is ultimately responsible for the recruitment of paid and unpaid staff that agrees with the church's core values, mission, vision, and strategy.
6. The Lead Pastor will encourage and provide opportunities for staff development.
7. The Lead Pastor will operate within applicable personnel policies that clarify personnel procedures for paid and volunteer staff.

Note: "Ultimately responsible" does not mean directly responsible. Other staff may hire people in their areas. However, final responsibility rests with the Lead Pastor (the "buck stops" with him).

Pastor's Board Responsibilities

The Lead Pastor will support and keep the board informed in its ministry.

1. The Lead Pastor will keep the board informed of any relevant trends, church issues, needs, external and internal changes, and problems that they should be aware of that are affecting or could affect the ministry positively or negatively.
2. The Lead Pastor will confront the board if he believes that it has violated its own governing policies and board-pastor policies in a way that is detrimental to its working relationship with him.
3. The Lead Pastor will provide the board with any information necessary for it to make fully informed decisions on the matters that come before it.

Pastor's Code of Conduct

1. The Lead Pastor is responsible to see that the church's ministries address the spiritual needs of its members and attenders.
2. The Lead Pastor will recognize the high visibility of his life and abstain from even the appearance of evil (1 Tim. 3:1–7; Titus 1:7–9; Rom. 14:1–23).
3. The Lead Pastor shall make sure that conditions for paid and volunteer staff are fair and supportive of their ministries.

4. The Lead Pastor will not show preference toward nor discriminate against any staff member who properly expresses dissent.
5. The Lead Pastor will not prevent staff from grieving to the board when internal procedures have been exhausted.
6. The Lead Pastor will protect staff from those who might seek to undermine them or their ministries in some way.

   - The Lead Pastor will confront such people.
   - The Lead Pastor will initiate church discipline of those that persist.

Note: Rather than a board-approved personnel manual, there is board policy on the treatment of personnel.

Pastor's Financial Management

1. The Lead Pastor has the responsibility for oversight of the church's finances.
   - The board is responsible only to make policies governing financial management and the monitoring of the pastor's funds management.
   - The pastor is responsible for funds management.

     ✦ The pastor will assign only approved personnel to handle the funds (a treasurer, a business manager, etc.).
     ✦ The pastor will oversee how those funds are handled (the collecting, counting, depositing, and accounting for all funds in a manner above reproach).

2. The Lead Pastor will lead the staff to create a budget for church approval that plans for the expenditure of the church's finances.

   • This plan reflects projected income and expenditures.
   • This plan informs all church ministries of their funding for the coming year.
   • This plan will reflect the church's strategic planning (facilities expansion, disciple making, church planting, etc.).

3. The Lead Pastor is responsible to raise the funds necessary to meet the budget.

   • The pastor and others will regularly cast the church's vision.
   • The pastor and others will preach on and teach biblical principles of giving at least on an annual basis.
   • The pastor and others will invite the people of Lake Pointe publicly and privately to invest in God's kingdom.
   • The pastor is responsible to see that the congregation is regularly informed of the church's financial condition.

4. The Lead Pastor will oversee the church's cash flow.

   • The pastor will monitor all income and expenses.
   • The pastor will communicate and account for all receipts and expenses to the board on a monthly basis.
   • Nonbudgeted expenditures by the Pastor should be reported to the Board within thirty days.

Nonbudgeted expenditures of more than $20,000 should have prior Board approval.

5. The Lead Pastor will manage staff compensation and benefits.

- The pastor will establish a compensation and benefits package that fairly reflects the staff's abilities, prior experience, and ministry position in the church.
- The pastor will establish a compensation and benefits package that is reasonable and affordable and is subject to the church's income.

  + The pastor may or may not automatically grant yearly cost of living increases.
  + The pastor may award bonuses and merit increases based on each person's yearly accomplishment of ministry performance goals and responsibilities.

Pastor's Asset Management

The Lead Pastor will oversee the church's assets so that they are properly protected and well maintained.

1. The Lead Pastor is ultimately responsible to make sure that the church is insured against any casualty or theft losses and against any liability losses to board members, staff, or the congregation.

2. The Lead Pastor is ultimately responsible for the maintenance and repair of the church's facilities and equipment in a timely fashion.

Pastoral Committees

Pastoral committees, when used, will support the Lead Pastor's ministry and never interfere with his relationship with the board or staff.

1. Pastoral committees may be temporary or ongoing and exist to help the Lead Pastor accomplish his ministry as determined by him. (Such committees might assist the pastor in strategic planning, budgeting, facilities evaluation, preparing personnel manuals, conducting environmental scans, and so on.)
2. Pastoral committees may not speak or act for the Lead Pastor or staff except when given such authority for specific and time-limited purposes.
3. Pastoral committees have no power and will not exercise authority over the pastor or any of his staff.

Pastor's Emergency Succession

The Lead Pastor will protect the church from the sudden loss of his services by recommending to the board and preparing at least one qualified person to lead in his place who is reasonably familiar with his duties.

Policies Governing the Board-Led Pastor Relationship

(The Board's Relationship with the Lead Pastor)

Pastor's Authority

The board corporately entrusts the Lead Pastor with the authority to be the primary leader of the church and its ministry.

1. The Lead Pastor answers only to the board when it acts corporately as the board.
2. The Lead Pastor as the primary, designated leader of the church has authority over individual board members except when they act corporately as the board.

   - The pastor may confront a board member over spiritual issues.
   - A board member will generally follow the leadership of the pastor when functioning on the board or serving in a church-related ministry.
   - The pastor will not tell a board person how to decide an issue that the board is addressing corporately.

3. The Lead Pastor and all board members including the chairman will minister together and relate to one another as if they are equals.

4. The Lead Pastor is not under the authority of the board chairman, any individual board member, any other board committee, or any individual in the congregation.

Pastor's Accountability

The board will hold the Lead Pastor accountable and responsible for his performance as well as for the performance of the church's paid and unpaid staff.

Pastor's Supervision

The board will supervise the Lead Pastor.

1. The board will draft written policies as needed that prescribe what the pastor may and may not do to accomplish the ministry's general direction (ends) and strategy (means). Additionally, as needed, the board will draft written policies that direct the pastor to accomplish biblically prescribed functions.

2. The board will design the policies so that they begin broadly and, where necessary, will be more specific in nature.

3. The board grants the pastor the latitude to interpret these policies within reason but retains the right to refine them further in areas of question or disagreement.

4. The board authorizes the pastor to draft all staff policies as he sees fit.

Pastor's Monitoring and Evaluation

The board will both monitor and evaluate the Lead Pastor's ministry performance.

1. The board will informally, regularly monitor the pastor's performance.
2. The board will facilitate a formal, annual evaluation of the pastor's performance.

   - The board will collectively evaluate the Lead Pastor's performance.
   - The Lead Pastor will conduct a self-evaluation and will receive an evaluation from his direct reports.

Notes

1. Seth Godin, *Tribes* (London, England: Penguin Books Ltd., 2008), 1

Chapter One

1. For more information about the Master's Program, go to www.mastersprogram.org.

2. Relational Fitness = Do I have same-gender close Christian friends who know me well and speak into my life to help me be my best self?

3. Jim Loehr and Tony Schwartz, *The Power of Full Engagement* (New York: Free Press, 2003).

4. John R. O'Neil, *The Paradox of Success: When Winning at Work Means Losing at Life* (New York: Jeremy P. Tarcher/ Penguin Publisher, 1993, 2004).

5. Steve Stroope and Kurt Bruner, *It Starts at Home* (Chicago: Moody Publishers, 2010).

6. Doug Sherman and William Hendricks, *Your Work Matters to God* (Colorado Springs: NavPress, 1987).

7. Tom Rath, *StrengthsFinder 2.0* (New York: Gallup Press, 2007).

8. See http://www.ministryinsights.com/purchase-lfys-profiles.php.

9. Two that may be accessed online at no charge: www.spiritualgiftstest.com and https://www.churchgrowth.org/cgi-cg/gifts.cgi?intro=1.

Chapter Two

1. Mark Buchanan, *The Rest of God* (Nashville: Thomas Nelson, 2006).

2. For more ideas about leveraging holidays and special occasions for faith discussions, check out *The Faith Box* by Lydia Randall, a kit to help parents create and record special moments in a child's faith journey. You can order *The Faith Box* at myfaithbox.org. Also see *It Starts at Home* by Kurt Bruner and Steve Stroope (Chicago: Moody Publishers, 2010).

Chapter Three

1. "Parents accept responsibility . . . but struggle with effectiveness." *The Barna Update*, May 2003.

2. Ibid.

3. See full list of participating churches by downloading a free summary of the Strong Families Innovation Alliance discussions at DriveFaithHome.com.

4. Faith@Home is Lake Pointe Church's emphasis encouraging parents to pass their faith on to their own children. A detailed description of our church's particular model is in a later chapter.

5. You can download a free executive briefing that summarizes all of the key discussions from the Strong Families Innovation Alliance at DriveFaithHome.com.

6. You can see samples from several of these campaigns by clicking the idea box at DriveFaithHome.com.

7. You can learn more about using the HomePointe model in your church and see samples from the growing network of churches at DriveFaithHome.com.

Chapter Four

1. Mark Chaves, *Congregations in America* (Cambridge, MA: Harvard University Press, 2004), 17.

Chapter Five

1. Steve Stroope and Aubrey Malphurs, *Money Matters in Church* (Grand Rapids, MI: Baker Books, 2007), 58–61.
2. Marcus Buckingham and Curt Coffman, *First, Break All the Rules* (New York: Simon & Schuster, 1999), 156.
3. Gordon MacDonald, *Renewing Your Spiritual Passion* (Nashville: Thomas Nelson, 1986), 71.

Chapter Six

1. John Carver, *Boards That Make a Difference* (San Francisco, CA: John Wiley & Sons, 2006).
2. Jim Brown, *The Imperfect Board Member* (San Francisco, CA: Jossey-Bass, 2006).
3. Larry Osborne, *Sticky Teams* (Grand Rapids: Zondervan, 2010).

Chapter Seven

1. Bill Hybels, *Axiom: Powerful Leadership Proverbs* (Grand Rapids: Zondervan, 2008).
2. Rick Warren, *The Purpose-Driven Church* (Grand Rapids: Zondervan, 1995).
3. See www.christianitytoday.com/ct/2006/october/5.25.html.
4. See www.frontlinedc.com.
5. See www.fbcrockwalltx.org.

Chapter Eight

1. You can order a video of our New Member Workshop and the New Member Workbook online at lpresources.lakepointe.org and click on Church Growth Resources.
2. Quote by Nicky Gumbel, Alpha Course.

Chapter Ten

1. These guidelines were created by the Lake Pointe Church staff in the late 1990s.

2. For more information on the D.I.S.C. personality profile, read *Leading From Your Strengths* by John Trent, Rodney Cox, and Eric Tooker (Nashville: B&H Publishing Group, 2004).

3. Read *StrengthsFinder 2.0* by Tom Rath (Washington, DC: Gallup Press, 2007) for a more complete description of what we call hard and soft strengths.

4. Nelson Searcy and Kerrick Thomas, *Launch* (Ventura, CA: Regal Books, 2006).

5. Dave Ferguson and Jon Ferguson, *Exponential* (Grand Rapids: Zondervan, 2010).

Chapter Eleven

1. Robert Simons, *Seven Strategy Questions* (Boston, MA: Harvard Business School Publishing, 2010), 25.

2. Based on members over the age of twenty-one. Age twenty-one is used because when members leave home to go to college, some retain their membership and we have no way to determine if they are givers, serving, or involved in missions.

Conclusion

1. Greg Hawkins and Cally Parkinson, *Reveal* (Willow Creek Association, 2007).

Appendix A

1. Mark Holmen summary of "American Religious Identification Survey 2001," found in *Building Faith at Home*, (Ventura, CA: Regal Books, 2007), 19–20.

2. Ibid.

3. David Kinnaman and Gabe Lyons, *unChristian: What a New Generation Really Thinks About Christianity* (Grand Rapids, Baker Books, 2007).

4. Ibid., 74.

5. Ibid., 248–50.

6. James Brandon Shields, *An Assessment of Dropout Rates of Former Youth Ministry Participants in Conservative Southern Baptist Megachurches* (Southern Baptist Theological Seminary Ph.D. Dissertation, 2008).

7. "Evangelism Is Most Effective Among Kids," *The Barna Update*, October 2004.

8. "Parents Accept Responsibility . . . But Struggle with Effectiveness," *The Barna Update*, May 2003.

9. Christian Smith and Patricia Snell, *Souls in Transition* (New York: Oxford University Press, 2009), 79.

10. Ibid., 246–48.

11. Ibid., 108–10, 214.

12. Ibid., 79.

13. Thom Rainer and Sam Rainer, *Essential Church* (Nashville: B&H Publishing Group, 2008).

14. Ibid., 3.

15. Mary Eberstadt, "How the West Really Lost God," *Policy Review*, Hoover Institute, June 1, 2007.

16. See http://marriage.rutgers.edu/Publications/SOOU/TEXTSOOU2006.htm.

17. Paul Asay, "Boomerang Believers," *The Gazette*, January 20, 2007.

18. Amy A. Kass and Leon R. Kass, *Wing to Wing, Oar to Oar* (Notre Dame, IN: University of Notre Dame Press, IN, 1999), 17.

Steve Stroope - *Lead Consultant and Coach*

PROVIDING CUSTOMIZED
HELP FOR CHURCHES
including:

-Capital Campaigns
-Strategic Planning
-Staffing
-Small Groups
-Church Finances
-Personal Coaching
-Missions
-Church Planting

For more information, contact:
steves@lakepointe.org
469-698-2249

Praise for *Tribal Church*

I've known Steve for fifteen years and he's the real deal. His life and leadership inspire me and so does the tribe of Lake Pointe Church. The straightforward, practical wisdom in this book will recalibrate any leader and any church at any stage of the game.

—Bill Hybels, senior pastor, Willow Creek Community Church, chairman of the board, Willow Creek Association

Steve Stroope has done us a favor by collecting three decades of experience into one book. Thank you, Steve, for living out an example of godly leadership.

—Max Lucado, pastor and best-selling author

Steve Stroope is more than knowledgeable about leadership and ministry. He is wise. He leads with strategic skill, discernment, and intuition. Every conversation with Steve has marked me and impacted my ministry; therefore, I am eager to read anything he writes.

—Eric Geiger, vice president of Church Resources Division at LifeWay Christian Resources and coauthor of *Simple Church*

Steve Stroope is the wisest and most effective pastor I know! This book is a treasure chest of godly wisdom for church leaders. Every pastor needs this book in their library.

—Nelson Searcy, lead pastor, The Journey Church, author, and founder of www.ChurchLeaderInsights.com

Steve Stroope is one of the most quietly influential voices in the growth and robustness of American Christianity. He is a collector of good ideas, what he calls "little things," the small but essential acts that cumulatively demonstrate the character of Christ in American church leadership. This book is by a leader I admire.

—Bob Buford, founder of Leadership Network and
The Buford Foundation and author of *Halftime*
and *Finishing Well*

Steve Stroope is one of the finest pastor-leaders of our generation. With a heart for local and global missions, Steve has modeled leadership methods that have been tested in the modern church world and can be great tools for equipping leaders in the days ahead.

—Bryant Wright, senior pastor,
Johnson Ferry Baptist Church, Marietta, Georgia